"Refreshingly candid yet laugh-out-loud funny. A terrific read!"

—Julia T.

"*Sharp Sticks* is an open and engaging portrait of marriage, motherhood, and life. Jackson's writing is fresh and honest- a voice that invites the reader to laugh, cry, and learn with her in each of her unpredictable stories."

—Jennifer M.

"I laughed out loud and I cried with depth and empathy. Kristie has the unique ability to be relatable. Plus she takes you right along on all her adventures."

—Melissa B.

"I really enjoyed *Sharp Sticks*. I consider a book well-written when it can make me both laugh and cry. It is great and worth buying extras to give as gifts!"

—Jenny T.

"Once I picked up *Sharp Sticks*, I couldn't put it down. It made me laugh and cry. I loved it!"

—Cassie J.

SHARP STICKS

ESSAYS OF *Embarassment*

AND REFLECTIONS ON *Redemption*

KRISTIE E. JACKSON

ISBN: 1461044383
ISBN-13: 978-1461044383

To my beloved husband, with unending gratitude

ACKNOWLEDGMENTS

I've been reluctant to write this acknowledgment, not because there is no one to acknowledge, but because there are so many.

My amazing dad, Roy Huber, inspired not only the title for this book, but much of what and how I write. My three sons, Will, Nate and Sam, are the most hilarious, sweet and insightful little guys I've ever had the pleasure of knowing, and I am tremendously blessed to have the daily stream of new material that they provide.

Initial reviewers of various essays included my treasured friends, Melissa Brown, Lindsay Hutter, Cassie Jakubowski, Brandi Laperriere, Kim Mislock, Kathie Napolitano, and Nancy Ziegler. Caitlin Staples, my much-adored niece, read early portions as well and authored the all-important description. My mom and my sister, Judy Huber and Laurie Staples, also read and edited early versions. Paige Bradshaw and Lori Louden both offered important affirmation at just the right time. Katie Cubba is my formatting angel; she repeatedly brought me back from the very edge of insanity. Jennifer Church designed the cover and has cheered on my writing pursuits for years. Emilie Zahurancik insisted on throwing me a book party where I did my first reading. That party was not only a lot of fun, but instilled greater confidence about moving forward with this print edition. The thoughtful feedback, encouragement, love and expertise of all these women kept me going.

Yet with my inherent lack of discipline this project never would have come to fruition without my husband's faithful proofreading, spot-on criticism and never-ending support. Will is my literary and grammatical rock, plus he *insisted* that I stick to self-imposed deadlines. I shamelessly lean on this incredible man in myriad ways and I am grateful that by God's abundant grace, he is able to prop me up, while remaining full of wit and wisdom.

I am humbled and honored by all of those who have so kindly reviewed *Sharp Sticks*. Brenda Solomon, Kerry Knott, and Carole Schryber are all dear friends and their descriptions of this book touch my heart and mean the world to me.

There are many others who have offered sweet words of encouragement to me over the years. To all of those who are not named here, may I say thank you from the bottom of my heart.

CONTENTS

INTRODUCTION

A couple of years ago I was in an airport with my husband, Will, and our three young boys, Will, Nate and Sam. Realizing that I was about to board a flight without anything to read, I rushed to the little bookstore near our gate and bought Nora Ephron's *I Feel Bad About My Neck*. With such a great title, it was the first thing that caught my eye, and I believe I was destined to buy this book because it put many things in motion. Sam slept almost that entire flight, the big boys watched a movie, and Will and I were both engrossed in our books (it is part of my husband's constitution that he would never, ever be caught without something to read). Ephron is funny and honest, and *I Feel Bad About My Neck* is a highly amusing, fast-paced read, at least until the last few essays where she reflects on loss and heartache. The ending, which seemed to imply that life is ultimately random and often meaningless, left me with a profound sadness.

Yet as I reflected on the book, a vision for my own writing began to take shape. I've always been willing to tell stories and share embarrassing moments, but my faith in Jesus Christ also informs my worldview and gives context and meaning to the dark days that invariably come. For years I'd been writing fiction and devotional pieces, but after reading Ephron's book, I started dabbling in essay writing and found it be a tremendously fun way to memorialize life with my husband and three sons. I've also found that God teaches me so much through the process of writing about and reflecting on the everyday events of my life.

Some of the essays in this book are intended to be lighthearted and fun, while others describe some of the most heart-wrenching events of my life. In all of them I see evidence of God's unconditional love and redemption. It is my fervent prayer that *Sharp Sticks* will be an entertaining read, but even more importantly, that it will paint a picture of the peace, freedom and joy that Jesus offers to each and every one of us.

SHARP STICKS

I'm an optimist, often in an absurdly unrealistic way. I'm constantly convincing myself that I'll be able to accomplish about forty hours of work in a single afternoon. And a couple of years ago, when my husband, Will, was doing a short tour of duty in Germany as an Army doctor, we decided that I would bring our young boys over for a visit. At the time our older son, Will the third, was three, and Nate was a precocious eighteen months.

At first the prospect of flying across the Atlantic, just the boys and me, seemed a bit daunting. But my optimism worked its way through the idea like yeast in dough, and by the time I boarded that flight I was convinced it would be a snap. The flight was due to take off at about five p.m., and I made sure the boys were especially tired that afternoon. My plan was practically foolproof. We'd watch a movie on my laptop, eat a little something, and then sleep our way to Europe. Let's just say things didn't turn out quite that well! Will was asleep before we ever left the gate, and Nate tried to set a Guinness record for sleeplessness in his age category. They never were asleep at the same time, so by the time we landed I was about to pass out from utter exhaustion. Of course it was worth it, even though about the only thing Will remembers is "castles so old they were falling apart."

Sometimes I take on more than I should, but really my optimism has been one of the great blessings of my life. Plus, it's just part of who I am, as the fourth child in a family of optimists. My dad, a mechanical engineer and fighter pilot, rarely faced a problem he couldn't solve. But even in circumstances that he couldn't possibly control, my dad had a consistent response: "Well, I guess it's better than a sharp stick in the eye."

It really didn't matter what happened. He was unflappable. Only God knows how many times I heard that refrain, "well, it's better than a sharp stick in the eye."

It becomes part of your subconscious, part of who you are. Because let's face it, what isn't better than a sharp stick in the eye?

And my mom had her own mantra. No matter how insurmountable the facts appeared my mom would say, "God knows all about it, Honey. It will all work out." It was amazing to see how often things really did fall into place. So that's the way we lived. Every circumstance was viewed in the best possible light, and when things didn't turn out the way we wanted, well then, God surely had His reasons.

My darling brother Craig, who looked something like JFK Jr., except cuter, manifested our family's optimism early on. Craig was a busy, busy little boy and could hardly stand to sit still.

This made those early elementary years slightly challenging. But one day he came home from school with exciting news.

"Guess what?" he said, just beaming with pride. "I'm the best reader in the slow reading group."

Indeed, we were a family of optimists.

And of course the greatest reason anyone has to face life with optimism is to know that they belong to Christ. Nothing frees the soul for joy, and for humor, like resting in the love and adoration of our Risen Lord.

What follows then are stories about sticks, some sharper than others.

HOW'S THE WEATHER UP THERE?

Are there any phrases that just make you cringe? I have one and it's not that it's offensive; it's more that I find it silly. Yet I've been asked how the weather is up here innumerable times in my thirty-nine years, the majority of which have been spent at just a hair under six feet tall. What is a good answer, anyway? Sunny and clear? Better than the weather down there in the land of absurd questions? I never have answered—I just smile awkwardly and try to escape. I've often wondered why it's even acceptable. I mean, can you imagine if I regularly asked short men whether they were once jockeys? Or fans of Napoleon? Yet I'm often asked if I played basketball or volleyball. It says a lot about how we, as a society, value height. Research reveals that tall people are more likely to be "successful" and that generally they make more money.

Of course, the prospect of success can be almost a consolation prize for growing up tall, because it's not always easy, especially for a girl. I remember well avoiding the colors green and yellow. The marketing campaign for the Jolly Green Giant and his vegetables was ubiquitous when I was in elementary school. If I wore too much green, I would be sure to hear the jingle, "bum, bum, bum, Green Giant!" And yellow? Well, it doesn't take too creative a mind to come up with "Big Bird." Even in my own family (where I was the only statistical giant), I was teased unmercifully. Once, when we were vacationing on the Atlantic coast of Florida, my brother, Craig, who was very loving most of the time, said, "Kristie, lay down."

"What for?" I asked, naively.

"Lay down, so we can walk on over to the Bahamas."

Yes, my long stick of a body was the butt of many jokes.

It took a long time before I was comfortable with my height. I longed for a girlfriend who also knew gianthood. Instead, I towered above all my friends. Once, when I was about seventeen, I did have a rare opportunity to make some tall friends, and it wasn't in a basketball or volleyball league. I was just in the mall, making my way to my favorite sales rack, when a gentleman about six-foot-eight and one-hundred-fifty pounds approached me with odd determination. I don't even think we made eye contact. He just handed me a business card, mumbled something like, "see you there," and speed-walked away.

I was sort of taken aback by the encounter and stood there for a moment before I looked at the card. When I read it, I was amused and horrified at the same time. On it was information about a local dance club/bar. The terms of entry were strict. No woman could get in unless she was at least five-foot-ten, and no man unless he was at least six-four. Although I have never been big on the bar scene, and never acted on the invitation, it was tempting. The idea of being average, or even (based on the fine beau who invited me) below average! I wondered what that would feel like.

What's amazing is how early we learn to identify what average is. With a six-foot-four husband, we were bound to have some rather tall offspring, and so far all three boys are consistently off the chart for height. One pediatrician really put it into perspective when our oldest turned four. He told us that Will the Third was in the 50th percentile—for a six year old.

So it really does present challenges, even for boys, because people's expectations are dramatically different. When my first son was two but looked more like four or five, I was tempted to have a little t-shirt made that said, "I'm TWO...Really!" Perhaps if people around me – especially those waiting near me in the grocery check-out line—realized he wasn't nearly as mature as he looked, they'd be more understanding when the inevitable tantrums were thrown.

One time when we were at the pool, a little girl about his size tried to play with him. She was probably about five or six and Will was two-and-a-half. She was trying to suggest little games they could play in the water, but she got mostly grunting noises in lieu of a response. At that time Will's vocabulary consisted of about twenty words. Although he could practically give the Gettysburg Address just by grunting and pointing—at least I understood him perfectly.

But the little girl by the pool wasn't quite so skilled at deciphering what it all meant, so in her frustration, she finally just looked at him bewildered.

"How old ARE you?" she demanded.

To my astonishment and horror he answered, "I'm two, but I'm huge."

It was his most complete statement (using actual words) that he had ever made. How often had he heard me explain away his height? It sounded almost like he was apologizing. Oh my darling! My huge, little darling!

I still field frequent questions about his height, and the height of his brothers, but I try to choose my words carefully. I never want them to feel like being tall is a bad thing. Nor do I want them to think that their height makes them superior. It's an uphill battle with the visuals that bombard us everywhere we go, but I want to my boys to reject the egregiously excessive value society places on outward appearances. A couple of summers ago I had a fantastic opportunity to address this issue head-on.

The boys and I were getting frozen refreshments at a place I need not name. Moments later Will, who was six at the time, timidly asked, "Was that a girl or a boy that waited on us?"

I told him that I wasn't exactly sure to whom he was referring since there were a couple different people at the counter. In truth, I was pretty certain which middle-aged woman had prompted the question.

After Nate had a tear-inducing spill, I let the two boys go back and order another one. Then we finished up our treats and went home.

I was upstairs when I heard Will's kind little voice on the steps.

"Mommy," he said, filled with sorrow. "There's something so sad about the girl that waited on us."

"Why don't you come talk to me about it."

Will came the rest of the way up the steps. I sat down on a chair and pulled him onto my lap.

"What was it, sweetheart? What was so sad about her?"

"I don't want to say," he answered, eyes downcast.

"Well, was it something about how she looked?" I asked.

He nodded.

"Well, do you know what the Bible says? It says that God looks at our hearts. Maybe she has a beautiful heart. That's what really matters – whether she's kind and sweet, whether she loves Jesus. You happen to be a very cute little boy, but you know what? That doesn't matter to God at all. What matters is your sweet nature. What matters is that Jesus lives in your heart."

This seemed to make him feel a little better. He was at least looking me in the eye. I guess that's what made him feel bold enough.

"She had a beard," he said without anything but compassion in his voice.

"She did? Aww, that is kind of sad, isn't it? I bet she probably has a beautiful heart though. Don't you think so?"

"Mm-hmmm," he answered, sliding off my lap and moving on. It had been plaguing him, but now he'd had enough of our weighty conversation.

I didn't bother to tell him about my fear, my fear that is not wholly irrational based on how often I find use for tweezers; my fear that I myself might one day be bearded.

Either way, I sure hope he remembers to love me for my heart.

DO NOT TRY THIS AT HOME

What I am about to tell you is a horrid tale. I mean it is truly ugly, not for those unwilling to look deep within their own hearts and admit that no matter how sanctified and pure it is, that this side of heaven there will always be a dark corner that's ever-willing to take over. And this story is definitely not for those who never lose their composure. It is such a gruesome story that I wish to death it wasn't true. And it is only after the passing of many, many years that I am tempted to find it just a tiny bit funny.

Will and I got married too young. Probably a lot of twenty-four year olds are perfectly capable of handling marriage – we just weren't among them. We each had the maturity of your average sixth-grader, and we were both terribly stubborn.

I brought many ridiculous notions down the aisle. For example, I really believed that Will should earn my respect. I waved that label above his head like he was some kind of a puppy. Here doggie, come on, jump. I also had a sick habit of pushing his buttons just to exhibit how much control I had over him (snide comments that disparaged Will's intelligence were sure to get a response). What's more, Will had the same bad habit and it was easy—all he had to do was utter the word "nag." We knew just how to set each other off and it was a mess. So I'm sure, given the fact that we're still married, that you already know that this is a story about grace. But friend, you have no idea. It gets worse.

One day when Will and I were working each other up into a lather, hurling insults about who knows what (the smallest of infractions would cause a blow-up), we witnessed the mercy of God in a new way. We'd both been stoking that crazy fire until Will, in a complete fury, and looking not unlike the Incredible Hulk, took his arms and swept them across my dresser. All my little trinkets crashed to the floor and a jewelry box I'd had since I was a child broke. I think a natural inclination would have been to weep, but instead I stormed out of the room, and I think right out of our little apartment.

But a few minutes later I started having this sense of resolve. He's never going to do that again, I told myself with great zeal and determination. Do you know the emphatic inner voice I'm talking about? The one whose name is Pride? Well, it's never good to listen to that voice. But I did. Intently.

Before our latest marital contest erupted, Will was preparing to study on our bed. He was in medical school and much of his time was spent in the same position. He'd prop up on his elbows and pour over his books by the hour, and I knew that's how I'd find him. Now I'm warning you, again, that this is not pretty, but I went to the kitchen and grabbed a wooden cutting board. Then I stealthily made my way to the bedroom. Will was lying there just as expected.

With the cutting board high in the air, and my presence unknown to Will, I must have looked like someone going after a giant fly. In a clearly deranged state of mind, I used all my strength to swat Will squarely on the bottom. I retreated with fear, evidencing at least some recognition that my scheme was truly dangerous. But all of a sudden, a most surprising sound flooded the whole apartment.

By God's abundant mercy, Will found his paddling to be downright hysterical. He laughed and laughed and laughed. He laughed until tears were streaming down his face.

I still shudder to think what could have happened, but I am happy to say that Will and I bear little resemblance to the married children playing with fire in that apartment. We just celebrated our 15th anniversary, and by God's grace we had only one cutting board incident. But among the myriad lessons that can be gleaned from our story, one stands out to me now more than ever. And that is that even though we are more mature, emotionally and spiritually, deep down we are still those people. I can't pretend that wasn't me with the cutting board. Will can't pretend he didn't do that Hulk move. It's humbling, but that's good. God loves a humble heart.

I am so thankful and so overwhelmed that God has removed our transgressions as far as the East is from the West. But even though God doesn't hold them against us, I believe our darkest personal memories can serve an important purpose. It is not about feeling guilt or shame, but about grappling with our own depravity. It's about recognizing our own dire need for redemption. As Jesus said, "It is not the healthy who need a doctor, but the sick" (Matthew 9:12). I need to remember that I'm sick. I don't want to take for granted what my salvation cost Him, and I don't want to forget how desperately I need the indwelling of the Holy Spirit. And perhaps most of all I want to remain ever-awed by God's grace.

WEDDINGS AND BURSTING DRESSES

It's kind of amazing that what I am about to tell you is true. I mean, I can understand someone bursting a dress once in her life, but twice?

My friend Melissa was recently in a wedding. When she went to get fitted for the bridesmaid's dress, she wanted to order a size smaller than they measured her for. The dress store put up a fight. They only agreed to order the smaller dress if Melissa signed a waiver of responsibility. But guess who had the last laugh? Melissa did. She was so motivated and worked so hard to get in shape for the smaller dress that when she went to pick it up they had to take it in!

But I am not Melissa, and I did not have the last laugh.

My oldest brother, Jeff, got married in 1992. I was twenty years old and I weighed about forty pounds less than I do now. I was almost too skinny, but I loved the way I looked and so I intended to wear a form-fitting, short black velvet dress to his wedding. To say that this dress was flattering is an understatement. It was the best I've ever looked in my whole life. My hair was long and I had ample time to spend curling it and putting on make-up.

My sister, Laurie, and I were getting ready at her house. Her husband had already left with my niece, Caitlin, since she was the flower girl in the wedding. Unfortunately, Laurie is not familiar with the word "early." Her constitution does not appear to allow a leisurely pace for anything. So she was taking rollers out of her hair about twenty minutes before the wedding twenty-five minutes away.

"Can you put Dane in the car?" she called, referring to her two-year-old son.

"Sure," I answered. And so I picked this handsome little guy up in my form-fitting velvet dress and high heels. But he began to scream and cry like I was abducting him or something.

I tried to console him as I carried him to the car. "Buddy, Mommy's coming. Honey boy, don't worry. Dane, she's coming!"

But he was not convinced. He was fighting me every high-heeled step of the way. My sister's car was parked on the edge of the driveway, so to get Dane into his car seat I had one foot on the cement driveway and one foot on the grass. As I tried to load him against his will, the adrenalin gave him the strength of Hercules and it was a vicious battle. As I buckled him in spite of his defensive backbend maneuver, I lost my balance and crashed to the ground. My beloved dress nearly fell off since the seam in the back ripped about twenty-five inches up from the slit.

I ran back into the house frantic.

"Laurie!" I called upstairs, bordering on hysterical. "Laurie!"

Her natural response was to think something happened to Dane and she came running to the top of the steps "What is it? Oh my gosh, what is it?" She was clearly petrified at what I was about to tell her, and the idea of something happening to Dane immediately sobered me.

"Oh no, he's fine. He's in the car. I just ripped my dress," I said calmly and turned around to show her.

"Oh no!"

We had to leave right then or else miss the wedding. Laurie was already going to have to use her Andretti mode to get us there. So I took my dress off, grabbed a stack of safety pins, and for some inexplicable reason grabbed the nearest article of clothing to wear en route. But the nearest article of clothing was a sweat-drenched yellow muscle shirt of my brother-in-law, Bob's, that he had worn earlier in the day to mow the grass. So I marched to the car in sexy black high heels, sheer black nylons, and a yellow muscle shirt decorated like confetti with blades of grass. The dress was strapless and didn't require a bra, so it was quite humorous that I chose a muscle shirt for modesty. I may as well have been naked from the waist up.

I cowered in the backseat with Dane and tried to pin the dress as best I could, but it looked beyond ridiculous. We remedied the situation by shuffling into the sanctuary like conjoined twins, my butt glued to her pelvis. And I've never been so glad to sit down in my life. Amazingly, between the ceremony and reception I visited a seamstress friend who sowed it up so perfectly that there would be no way anyone could tell the damage wrought an hour before.

So you might think I would've learned my lesson. But you'd be wrong.

In August of 1999, my oldest friend in the world and cousin, Cassie, got married. I sent in measurements for my dress since I lived in Arlington, Virginia and the wedding was in Michigan. I probably sucked in my stomach a little too much for the measurements or maybe ate a little too much at the rehearsal dinner. Either way, I was a disaster the day of her wedding. A disaster. It's actually not even funny to me like the first dress bursting. It still gives me a sick feeling, like I could cry about it all over again.

Will and I were getting ready to leave for the wedding from my sister's house when I realized that I didn't have my shoes. A few mental steps back and I realized I had left them in Cassie's car. Not that big of a deal, we'd swing by and get them. But when we went by her house just a mile or two away, the car was locked. Her dad was still at home, but he didn't have keys to the car. This is when I started to panic. I pictured myself ruining Cassie's wedding by walking down the aisle barefoot.

I started bawling my eyes about it. Neither my husband nor my uncle understood why I found this so devastating, but I think it was because I didn't want my own persistent buffoonery to take away from Cassie's day. Most of the time I'm okay living with my scatterbrained idiocy, but to impose that on Cassie on her wedding day made me feel like a complete loser. My tears, which were flowing like a faucet, were tears of profound shame. I think I was worried that my carelessness would naturally imply a lack of concern. And the truth of course is and was that I could not possibly love Cassie any more than I do. So we raced to the church and stopped at Kohl's en route. Will pulled up to the front door, and I ran in, sobbing loudly like some kind of a lunatic. I grabbed a pair of shoes that weren't exactly beautiful, but would at least avoid a barefoot matron of honor. The cashier, not knowing what to say or do, just asked, "Are you okay?" I nodded and ran out. But the day's buffoonery had just begun.

At the church my mom tried to help me gain my composure and get dressed. But the zipper on my dress, which had previously been sticking just would not unzip. I mean I tried. She tried. I think my dad even tried. The only reason Will didn't try was because I sent him back to Cassie's house twenty minutes away to fetch the shoes. I could feel the tears welling up again, but now Cassie was there too, and I had to keep myself together. I told my mom in a firm voice, "you are going to have to pull it over my head."

This was not easy, and it made her terribly nervous to do it, but we had no choice. There was a lot of pressure exerted on that seam but it held up and I was ecstatic to have it on. Then two minutes before I needed to walk down the aisle, Will arrived with my shoes. All was well. For now.

Cassie and her husband, Michael, did a lot of moving around during the ceremony. They lit candles, they knelt down, they got up. I was perplexed, as the Matron of Honor, about how often I was supposed to straighten out her dress, which had a substantial train. I erred on the side of aesthetics and made it look as pretty as I could, every time she moved. That meant I was putting a lot of pressure on my trusty seam. Every time I bent over it probably got a little closer to bursting forth.

But by God's abundant, abundant mercy and grace, the actual dress explosion occurred during pictures. It was quite embarrassing, but not nearly as humiliating or ruinous as it would've been during the wedding ceremony.

Will and I stopped on our way to the reception at a dry cleaners that did alterations, but they were unwilling to mend the dress. Instead, it was safety pin time once again. Will and I did the conjoined-twin shuffle into the reception so late that the best man speech had already been given, and I sat down next to the beautiful bride and stayed in my seat for the duration. I did not go the bathroom. I did not socialize. I sat there, my safety-pinned bottom glued to my seat.

Not my finest hour, but worth remembering because God loves a humble heart. And thinking back to that day, now eleven years ago, but as vivid as yesterday, is totally incompatible with pride. Some days when I am thinking of myself more highly than I ought, I should be deliberate in retrieving this memory. Because it fills me with gratitude for the timing of the bursting, and makes me realize just how much of a buffoon I really am. Incredibly, my husband still loves me. Cassie still loves me. My brother and his wife still love me. Most of all, the Creator of the Universe loves me with an undying, unconditional, unquenchable love. And I live in the security that He will keep loving me no matter what I do.

A VERY SHARP STICK

My dad's philosophy of "better than a sharp stick in the eye" served me quite well for many years. It is patently true in the face of almost every obstacle, injustice or grievance.

Getting an insultingly measly tip after waiting on a demanding group of restaurant patrons the entire night? *Better than a sharp stick in the eye.*

Innocently sitting at a stoplight in my cute new car and getting smashed into by a woman running a red light? *Better than a sharp stick in the eye.*

Taking the law school entrance exam while just outside the window a construction vehicle clattered and banged and beeped, seemingly in reverse for a solid three hours? *Better than a sharp stick in the eye.*

Splitting my dress in half twenty minutes before my brother's wedding? *Better than a sharp stick in the eye.*

But the night of November 6, 1999, I would've opted for a sharp stick. And my memories of that day remain mercilessly vivid. More than eleven years have passed, and I still have absolute clarity over minor details, like the CD I was listening to in the car as I ran errands, preparing for my parents' arrival later that night. Elated to be a homeowner, I darted from place to place, savoring the unseasonable warmth and the last colors of fall. A week earlier my husband, Will, and I had closed on our first home, a garden-style condo in Reston, Virginia. We had moved from a high-rise apartment in Arlington, just steps from the Metro, twenty miles west, where you could see the faint outline of the Blue Ridge Mountains.

That little place, two bedrooms and two baths spread over three levels, had seen better days. But its state of disrepair made it affordable, and its basic structure was adorable, with an open floor plan, and an abundance of light. The gas fireplace, garage, and small deck made it even better. It just needed some work. Well, lots of work. Sloppy painting was among its most obvious problems; it looked as if it were inspired by a monochromatic Jackson Pollock. Huge globs of paint were strewn about, and frozen streams of paint ran down the spindles on the staircase. If you closed your eyes and ran your hand over the railing, you'd know the paint job was intended to be a mockery. The carpeting was not terribly worn, but there were numerous areas where someone had burned holes in it, presumably with a cigarette. Such destructive acts are almost commonplace now, but this wasn't a foreclosure, and we never learned why our four-year-old condo was in the condition it was; we were just thrilled to be able to afford it. My parents were instrumental in helping me find it – the three of us had spent countless hours condo-shopping while my husband worked long hours in the hospital, and my dad was excited to help us whip it into shape.

My sister, Laurie, has been a flight attendant for more than twenty years, and this has been a huge blessing for my whole family. My mom and dad could fly anywhere for free or a nominal fee, and they utilized the privilege with regularity. Hardly a month would pass without them going somewhere. That balmy Saturday afternoon in November, I thought about calling my parents to reconfirm our plan. It had been a couple of days since I had spoken to them, but I knew they'd call if something changed. I would pick them up at Washington National at about eight. I'd call to make sure the flight was on time, and I'd be there at the curb to get them. At the time, my parents lived in Juno Beach, Florida, and they were flying from Palm Beach to D.C. via Detroit, which may seem a bit odd, but at that time, all of Northwest Airlines flights connected through Detroit, Memphis or Minneapolis.

Will was in his third year of internal medicine residency at Walter Reed Army Medical Center and was on call that day, which meant he was doing a twenty-four hour shift in the hospital. I was in my third year of law school at George Mason University, but I didn't crack a book that day. I focused instead on clearing pathways through the boxes and getting ready for my parents. I put clean towels in their bathroom and made up their bed. I had the windows open and I was just giddy about how cute and welcoming the guest room looked.

But about five minutes before I needed to leave for the airport, the phone rang. It was my brother, Craig.

"Have you talked to Mom?" he asked.

"No," I answered, thinking for a brief instant that maybe they had missed their connecting flight from Detroit.

"I'm so sorry, Kristie, I am so, so sorry. But Dad had a heart attack on the plane."

I dropped to my knees and started to scream, but after a few panicked seconds, I gained my composure to ask, "Well, how is he?"

Then I heard my brother break down on the other end, "I'm so sorry, honey, I'm so, so sorry, but he didn't make it."

I slammed the phone down and started screaming at the top of my lungs. I was on my knees, face to the floor next to my bed. I wailed there, flinging myself up and down and banging my fists on the floor, screaming and screaming and screaming.

Then I grabbed the phone and paged Will with a 911 ending. He called seconds later, and I sobbed and screamed into the phone, "My dad died!" It was as if I didn't know how to express my new reality. It felt cold and detached and harsh to scream those words, and I could hardly believe I was uttering them. Ninety seconds before I had been hurriedly tidying up a few loose ends, getting ready to walk out the door to see my parents. And now I was telling my husband that we would never see my dad alive again.

Will said he'd come home right away and we hung up. I continued my sobbing on the floor and I remember my simple prayer that I spoke aloud. "God help her. Please, please help her." From those first moments, I thought losing my dad would be like losing both my parents. I didn't see how my mom could possibly be my mom without my dad.

I talked to my brother Craig again and he told me that Dad had been taken by ambulance to a hospital near the airport in Detroit. It was a hospital that my dad had taken me to when I was little and my mom was out of town. I was having stomach pain and they were evaluating me for appendicitis. I can still picture the inside and outside of this hospital perfectly, even though that's the only time I was ever there. Now I couldn't help envisioning my distraught mom in its hallways. Since my brother, Jeff, and sister, Laurie, both lived nearby at the time, they met my mom in the ER. My mom told me later that leaving my dad there that night was the hardest thing she has ever had to do.

I was crying and pacing the floor of our condo when the police knocked on the door, which wasn't too terribly surprising. After all, I had been screaming my head off with all the windows open. But it was still a surreal experience. They asked to see my license, and I offered to let them look around, but I don't think they doubted my explanation. They kindly offered to stay with me until Will got home, or to call someone for me, but I told them I would be fine. After a little while they left and I sat on the steps to our front door until Will pulled up.

What was he to say? What could he do? Yet I was so thankful to have him home. Will and my dad had always had a fantastic relationship, full of mutual admiration and respect. Will was stunned at his own loss and brokenhearted for me. We booked the first flight out in the morning to meet up with the rest of my family.

We sat on our bed and Will prayed with me and tried reading Scripture to me. He held me in his arms, but I was numb and restless. Finally, Will was drifting off to sleep and so I went and sat on the bed where my parents were supposed to be. I thought about how quickly my life had changed. I stared at the ceiling until it was time to pack and leave for the airport. I was filled with dread about seeing my mom. I was sure that with a shattered heart, she wouldn't even look the same.

Will and I landed in Detroit the next morning before eight o'clock. I remember standing at the curb, waiting for our ride, half expecting my dad to pull up, smiling his wide and winsome smile and apologizing for all the confusion. But he didn't.

We went to my sister's house, and after a time of stunned and bewildered conversation, my mom was at the door. She had stayed the night at my uncle's, and all my fears were realized when I saw her. She looked twenty years older and even appeared frail. Devastation was evident in every square inch, and in that moment it didn't seem feasible that she would ever laugh again, or even smile.

But laughter in our darkest days is not impossible, and it provides hope and therapy for the soul.

My brother Craig and his wife, Tamara, also flew in that morning from their home in Jupiter, Florida, and so my mom was surrounded by all four children, their spouses and both grandchildren (my sister's daughter and son). My mom's brother also lived just up the road, and my aunt and uncle spent a large portion of that day with us. We mostly just sat around my sister's family room, talking quietly, still in a state of shock. And

I was finally able to get some rest, which in the midst of such grief is vital.

The next day was spent caravanning around, making arrangements for the funeral and burial. This decision process is an odd one, but I remember sitting around a large conference table at the cemetery. There were glimpses that afternoon of our real personalities, hints of the good-natured banter that usually characterized our time together. Then, for whatever reason, we were teasing my mom about her legendary modesty, and all of us were finding it humorous. As was the usual course, our resident comic, Craig, took hold of the conversation. Craig was always known for his quick wit, and it felt good to laugh. To hear my mom's laugh was a particular comfort. Craig just kept on, one-upping himself with one line after another. We were practically falling out of our seats laughing.

But then the cemetery representative abruptly came back into the conference room. Prudish and middle-aged, she looked perplexed, "Mmhh, joyful family," she said, sapping the mirth from the room and leaving us all feeling inappropriate, disrespectful and defensive. Instantaneously, my mom was back to tears.

A few minutes later, when the woman left the room again, Craig feigned outrage and acted out an imaginary confrontation. "Joyful family?" he mocked. "Joyful family? You insensitive whore! We'll show you joyful! Joyful and violent." To use those words as a punch line you need perfect comedic timing, and a kind and gentle spirit. In fact, Craig Huber might have been the only person ever who could take that moment and those words and combine them into something absolutely hilarious, and yet I'm sure it's one of those moments that you really had to be there to fully appreciate. In *The Divine Conspiracy*, Dallas Willard argues that shared laughter is a vital part of true community (New York: Harper Collins, 1997) p. 238. Although it may sound somewhat harsh to an outsider, that's really what "you insensitive whore" was all about. It was needful and memorable and funny, and is still repeated with great amusement a decade later.

Humor is a gift, a reprieve from pain. Of course, it requires balance. A person who is unable to be serious is tiresome and unattractive. That exchange in the conference room proved that this group of broken mourners was still my family, that we had not forever lost the unifying joy of sharing a laugh. Even though that moment was short-lived, it was a glimmer of normalcy in the midst of almost unbearable sorrow.

And we knew my dad would have wanted it that way. Nine months earlier, I had been sitting with my dad on the porch of their condo, overlooking the Atlantic Ocean. I was there to attend another funeral, the funeral of my mom's sister. My Aunt Janet had passed away a couple of days before, after a long and courageous battle with cancer.

"I know Mom is sad right now," he said. "It's her sister and she'll miss her, but if we *truly* believe what we *say* we believe, funerals should be parties. I want my funeral to be a celebration."

And in some respects his funeral was a celebration. It helped that we didn't watch him suffer, and he didn't have unfinished business or unresolved conflicts. He'd lived life to the full, and he was whisked away, having long professed faith in Jesus Christ. It didn't feel like a tragedy for Roy Lee Huber – his sixty-seven years were filled with blessing and marked by accomplishment.

He had earned a mechanical engineering degree from Michigan Tech and over the course of his career he obtained many patents and received many engineering awards. He also played high school and college football, and I can hear him telling Will that he used to hit like Ronnie Lott; he made this claim with a big, hearty laugh, but I've seen footage and I think he probably did hit something like Ronnie Lott. When he was done with school, he fulfilled his childhood dream of becoming a fighter pilot. My Uncle Jack told me that during World War II he and my dad used to stack hay in a field near the airport. Fighters and bombers like the B-17, P-38 and B-25 would fly overhead. Some were so low that they could wave to the nose and tail gunners and they would wave back. Twenty years later my dad and my uncle were both fighter pilots.

After pilot training, my dad came home and fell in love with the little girl next door, literally. My dad married my mom when he was twenty-six, and she was seventeen. The year was 1959 and my mom, Judy Cummins, was a beautiful child bride, just a few weeks out of high school. Five months before his death, my parents celebrated forty happy years of marriage by taking a special trip out west, visiting Yellowstone National Park.

His life left us with much to celebrate and the visitation nights at the funeral home were packed with people. Although the room was quite large, doors had to be opened to let in some air. I loved hearing stories about my dad and meeting some of his old friends. I had brought some extra clothes for my mom to wear, knowing that she hadn't packed funeral attire to come work on our beat-up condo.   I remember how fabulous she looked in my gray suit. I know my dad took pride in my mom's good looks and she made him proud by greeting everyone with grace and remarkable beauty.

At the funeral itself, both my brothers spoke. Their stories painted a great and true picture of my dad. The church was the one my parents had both grown up in, and it was where I grew up and was baptized as well. The pastor had known our whole family for years, and his message was personal and gospel-centered.

My dad would've been pleased, because although there was a flood of tears, it felt like a celebration too. Craig told about the time my dad tried windsurfing. Although we lived in Michigan, my parents had gone to Florida to celebrate their 25th anniversary with their good friends, Glady and Doug. My dad was fifty-one and Doug just a few years younger, but they were both athletic and game for adventure. The problem was that there was no wind. They both spent the entire afternoon fighting with their boards and sails, never catching a breeze or moving more than a few feet from where they started.

When they returned the equipment, the woman behind the counter said, "You know, next time, you might want to think about a lesson."

My dad didn't skip a beat. "Listen," he said, "when I'm down here on vacation, I'm here to relax. I don't have time to be *giving* any lessons."

So that was my dad, and my world would never be the same.

INVISIBLE BLANKETS AND GOOD
SAMARITANS

The weeks and months after my dad's death were miserable, exhausting and long. From Michigan, my mom went back to Florida with my three siblings in tow for support, and I went back to Virginia, hoping to pick up my studies and graduate on time. But wherever I went I wore the "invisible blanket" that C.S. Lewis talked about in *A Grief Observed*. I longed for people to acknowledge my pain or perceive how fundamentally the world had changed. Instead, life marched on all around me. Staying focused on anything was a tremendous challenge and as Thanksgiving and Christmas approached, I wanted to hibernate. It was a testament to God's grace that I passed my classes that semester – I remember writing a paper concerning Chinese economics. But it seemed so utterly meaningless to me. Everything I did felt like navigating through a heavy, persistent and apathetic fog.

Will and I were in church almost every Sunday, yet we knew nothing of true biblical community. I sat in church, my head hung low and my heart broken, and no one around me knew. When we first moved to the DC area in 1997 we went to a great church, Columbia Baptist, where we were warmly welcomed by a young marrieds Sunday school class. We were blessed immensely by the leaders of that class, Norman and Sue. They were genuinely interested in knowing us, and although they were busy with Norman's demanding job, which involved traveling around the world, they included us and loved us from the start. In fact, Norman provided vital professional connections for me, passing along my resume to the name partner of the law firm I eventually joined. But after we had attended Columbia for about a year and were contemplating church membership, I insisted that we try McLean Bible Church. I kept hearing about its pastor, Lon Solomon, so I thought we should check it out before we formally joined Columbia. It ended up that Pastor Solomon was even more remarkable than the rave reviews I'd heard, and after a few visits, I was convinced that McLean Bible should be our church home.

The teaching of McLean Bible Church was and is phenomenal, but it is a very large church. If you are not involved in a small group, you are anonymous. And while anonymous is never healthy, my anonymity was particularly ill-timed. Will was a medical resident, often working ninety hours a week or more (limits on work-week hours are now a condition of residency accreditation), and I was a law student reading untold hours every day just to keep up. I was also doing an internship with the Commonwealth Attorney's Office in Arlington. We knew no one in our neighborhood, and we each commuted a minimum of an hour to an hour and a half each day. I did not have a single believing friend from church or Bible study investing in me, speaking truth into my life, or praying with me. I do not share this to invoke pity. The blame for this unhealthy isolation fell squarely on my shoulders, and I knew that. I had not sought biblical community, believing that my schedule did not allow for anything else. With less than a year left of school, my goal had been to tread water until I reached the end. In a sense, my lack of godly friends was a calculated choice. Oh, but what a poor one.

And Will tried to be supportive. It helped me to know how much he loved my dad. They had been instant friends, and I think part of it was that they shared an uncommon intellect and were both extremely driven. They had an easy companionship, often spending hours together on the porch of my parents' condo, alternating between reading their books and discussing everything from sports to medical innovation to politics. They respected and enjoyed one another immensely. What a gift that was to me!

But despite his admiration for my dad, Will was not well equipped to shepherd me through my dark and lonesome days. He had never experienced such loss and I think he struggled with how to help me. Although I never voiced it, I can remember feeling irritated when Will would kiss me on the cheek over and over again. It must sound terribly trite to have been annoyed by his tender compassion, but in the moment, those loud and frequent kisses felt absurdly out of place. And our conversations in those first weeks hovered on the surface, when I longed for them to be deep and probing.

I don't know where I got my expectations about how things should be. And I didn't even know what exactly my expectations were, I just knew whatever they were, they weren't being met. Not that I said much. I hardly talked or even cried. I had a few meltdowns where I would cry for hours, but they never seemed to help, and if I tried really hard I could mostly keep my composure.

I remember wanting to blame someone for my dad's death. Maybe the airline should have made an emergency landing. Or maybe there should have been defibrillators on board the plane. I wanted to be angry at someone, and so it even bothered me that the airline didn't offer any condolences. There was no acknowledgement of any kind that a person had died on one of its flights, and that struck me as odd and irksome. Yet how could I possibly be angry when God's hand was so patently in the details? The mere thought of the same thing happening on the flight to National instead of Detroit was enough to bring me back to gratitude. Yes, my dad's death was sudden and entirely unexpected, but it was also peaceful and the fact that it was in Michigan was an amazing and unlikely provision.

So I didn't stay mad, but I did stay scared. I was scared that something would happen to Will, and I was scared of a possible intruder. I felt scared almost all of the time, and for almost no reason. Will worked overnight a couple times a week, and the more I was alone the more I became bionic in my hearing. Any sound from any of the three levels would jar me awake, and I was having more and more difficulty falling asleep. Finally, I bought a loud box fan for our bedroom. It blocked out all the random creaks and squeaks around the house and helped me rest.

We made it through the holidays, visiting Florida after Christmas. My grandparents drove down from their home three hours north, and the time together softened the ache. Each night we all piled into my mom's condo. We reminisced and shared meals and talked about the sufficiency of God's grace and of all the ways He had provided for us. We did not grieve as those without hope, and I was a different person there, a person more hopeful than afraid.

But in January school resumed, apathy set in, and although I passed those spring classes, I learned very little. My mock trial class was taught by a real judge and was held in his courtroom late in the evening. I had to be among the worst trial lawyers he'd ever seen, and a huge weight was lifted off my shoulders when the gavel fell for the last time on my case, not because I did an even moderately decent job, but because it was over. Somehow losing my dad had seriously impaired my capacity for stress. During my second year of law school, when high pressure interviewing is a part of daily life, I developed a nervous twitch in my eye, and even occasionally in my lip. But this was different, in both form and severity. This was full-body, full-spirit stress, infecting me from head to toe and centering on my chest, where I felt the crushing weight of a giant boulder all day long.

Plus, there were constant reminders that my dad was gone – all I had to do was look around the room – the condition of our humble abode was evidence of his absence. When my dad's suitcase was unpacked, it contained only a few articles of clothing, because it was so full of tools. And although I never actually saw his bag, I often pictured it flopped open on the bed, tools spilling out. This image pierced my heart over and over again.

The invisible blanket was lightest on days when I made reluctant steps toward normalcy. At the first sign of spring, we bought a grill for our deck, and I found the perfect bistro dining set. Many evenings we sat outside, grilling dinner or just having a glass of wine. Will often talked about my dad. He'd say things like, "Roy would've this or would've that." And he'd ask questions too. He could not have known how much that meant to me. Many beat the path of avoidance, rationalizing that bringing up the deceased will only upset the person further. But that is so misguided. In fact, I felt unloved by those who danced around my sorrow. How could someone who truly cares about you ignore your broken heart? It's not unlike The Parable of the Good Samaritan, with wounds that are emotional instead of physical. As in Jesus' example, the people you might expect to reach out to you, do not, and it is often surprising who is willing to go outside their comfort zone or be inconvenienced. Jesus' definition of "neighbor" is broad, and in my experience good neighbors are people who engage even when it's not entirely comfortable or easy to do so.

It's not that a person's sorrow needs to dominate conversation. It is not even necessary for the loss to be a common or recurrent topic; it just shouldn't be taboo. And people worry about what to say, but they shouldn't. The need is for acknowledgement, not for wisdom or a solution. The message can be simple: "I'm sorry for you. I'm praying for you." I liked hearing specific things too, like "I loved your dad's laugh" or "I remember the time when...," but any recognition is appreciated.

Grief is an inescapable part of life on earth. I hope when I encounter those who mourn – wrapped in their invisible blankets – that I fight off the instinct to pass on the other side. Instead, may I be like the Good Samaritan, willing to show compassion, even when it costs me something.

A LESSON IN SIMPLICITY

In 2006, my husband started a new job requiring our family to move from the Washington, D.C. area to Florida. Eighteen months later we moved back. Through this rather complicated process, my whole family learned some important lessons.

My eldest son, Will, learned the invaluable lesson of making friends wherever he goes. He went to preschool in Virginia, preschool in Florida, and then did half a year of kindergarten on either side of our move. So at the age of six he had gone to four different schools. Of course, from his perspective, this was totally normal. He thought schools were just something you sampled for a brief stint. So you can imagine how wonderful it was to hear that he loved that fourth school so much that he wanted to stir things up and go back there again!

Lessons were also learned from the stark contrast of two very different cultures. In Florida, we were blessed, like most of our neighbors, to live in a single-family home. We even had a gate to our community, ensuring a quiet and private little enclave. The population density in Greater Washington means single-family homes are the exception to the rule, and initially we lived in a condo roughly half the size of our house in Florida. The boys, however, thought the condo was bigger and better. After all, it was taller!

As for my husband and me, we gained a new appreciation for movers. The guys who moved us were incredibly hard workers. To think that our move was behind us in the course of a few days, but the guys who loaded and drove the truck spent three hundred days of the year packing, unpacking or hauling people's stuff. It's backbreaking, underappreciated work, and our esteem for those who do it couldn't be higher.

Will and I also learned that renting is an underutilized option. We never should have bought a home in Florida, until we were sure we were staying there. Three years after moving back to DC and we still own that house. Since we bought at the tippy-tippy-top of the market in April of 2006, we may never unload that house. We've been seriously schooled in housing economics and are extremely grateful for long-term renters who take good care of the house.

But of all the lessons we learned, the most important was the wonder of simplicity. Since we still had hopes that our house would sell, when we moved back, we decided to leave most of our things behind. Given our much smaller space, we brought only the essentials. For five months we lived without our HD television, without our comfortable overstuffed furniture, without all but a few pots and pans. Beanbags were a major source of seating and our young boys were without most of their toys and their beloved bunk beds. Instead our nighttime routine became "brush your teeth, put on your pajamas, and blow up your bed." And the wonderful thing was we were happy. We were content. Life was simple.

When our things finally did arrive, I was glad to have the boys sleeping in real beds again. But there was also something sad about throwing away their tattered air mattress. It meant the end of an era in which we spent much less time acquiring and caring for things. I don't think we need to go without beds to fight against the materialistic mindset of our culture. But I do believe we benefit from recognizing there is a fight. We need to be mindful that advertisements always aim to make us feel discontent. We have to be intentional if we hope to maintain any semblance of simplicity.

Paul knew the secret of being content: his circumstances were irrelevant. His Savior gave him strength in any and every situation, in need or when there was plenty. Like most Americans, my family doesn't understand what it means to be in need. All we know is plenty. Yet it is a blessing to have had even the tiniest corollary of Paul's Spirit-filled wisdom played out in our lives. In terms even my little boys can understand: things do not make you happy.

THE END OF THE BRITISH

I've heard people say that in every oral communication there are at least three distinct messages. There is the message the speaker intends, the message actually conveyed, and the message the individual hears. I saw the truth of this principle at work when I took my three little boys to Fort McHenry a few years ago. Fort McHenry is a lovely national monument about an hour from our home and is where Francis Scott Key penned the words to the Star-Spangled Banner. Our visit there was quite educational. I had always thought our anthem was written during the Revolutionary War, but now I know better and my little boys know better. It was written in 1814, during the Battle of Baltimore, when the British attacked Fort McHenry.

I have to admit that I was rather pleased with myself and with them that afternoon. On our drive home Will, who was six, and Nate, who was four, were spouting out all manner of facts and figures regarding the War of 1812. The recitation put Baby Sammy to sleep, and I had a surge of pride over my budding history buffs. Their level of interest and seeming comprehension was remarkable.

But then came bedtime. Nearing tears Nate told me he was afraid to go to sleep because "those bad guys with the cannons might come back."

"You mean the British?" I asked, trying not to laugh too uproariously.

Nate nodded gravely.

"Sweetheart, there is absolutely no chance of the British attacking us again," I offered. But big brother found my assurances wanting, wholly inadequate.

"Nate," he said, tenderly, "don't you remember? The Americans won. The British can't attack us again. We killed them all."

So much for history lessons! It provided a good laugh, but could the message received be more different than the message intended? And how often do we fail to discover that the little ones in our lives, or even the adults, have so misconstrued our message that they effectively believe we've wiped out the British race?

Our communication skills remain pitifully poor even though we communicate all day, every day, and I believe effective communication has an element of chemistry. There is an expressive connection with some people that goes beyond words, tone and body language. It helps to know someone well, but sometimes this ease of communication is immediate. Have you met someone new who is on your same expressive wavelength almost instantaneously? Someone you understand almost innately? That's communication chemistry.

I have a friend like this. We have spectacular chemistry. In fact I've told her that in terms of a quality/quantity ratio, she's my best friend. But we hardly ever see each other. She has four children, about a million friends, and she's highly invested in some really wonderful causes. Getting our schedules to align is almost impossible, but it actually doesn't matter how often I see her. Because I can spend five minutes with her and grapple with some profound issue and also share a wonderful laugh. Friendship is not about efficiency, but if it was, our kindred spirits could serve as the model.

But being understood is a vital and universal need. Self-deprecating humor is a way of life for me. But all is lost when the hearer doesn't share my communication chemistry. If I am poking fun at myself and the response is "awww," I feel robbed. Nothing ruins a funny moment like pity. For example, when I joke about proudly wearing a fabulous new sweater only to find at the end of the day that the 2 x 5 inch sticker identifying the size was never removed, I don't want someone to think the Large, Large, Large, Large, Large I was branded with all day is sad. I want them to join me in finding it hilarious that I could do such a thing.

And when you tell a friend with the right chemistry that you're stressed or tired, they know just what you mean, even though these are very subjective ideas. Consensus about words can be built over time, and we should be patient and long-suffering in this endeavor, but we should also be filled with gratitude when this mutual understanding is effortless.

Shopping can bind women together in interesting ways. Although at my current stage of life and weight, this is not my definition of fun. It's hard to find time for a leisurely trip to the mall and those fluorescent dressing room lights are just too cruel. But in the past (and hopefully in the future) shopping was great fun and separated the friendship wheat from the chaff. A true friend is consistently honest. When she says she loves an article of clothing you are trying on, you can trust it's a winner. If she says, "I'm not crazy about it," you know that you should never ever be caught dead in it. Solomon was so right when he wrote, "A lying tongue hates those it hurts, and a flattering mouth works ruin" (Proverbs 26:28). Who wants to go shopping with a lying flatterer?

Yet that doesn't mean there's no place for diplomacy. Diplomacy is imperative. Last winter my family went skiing. The ski school called us about Sammy, who was then three-and-a-half.

"Sammy could probably use a pep talk if you wanted to swing by and see him," they said. A pep talk? Surely this was code for "your son is being an uncooperative little monster," but I greatly appreciated the wisdom of this news bearer who chose words that conveyed the message with grace and dignity. Likewise, shopping with someone who tells you, "that dress makes you look fat as a butcher's dog," is not a friend, even if the dress makes you look exactly that. In short, diplomatic honesty equals wheat; brutal candor, chaff.

But whether we are at the mall or not, we should just resign ourselves to the fact that communication takes work, that we are imperfect at it, and that everyone we know is imperfect at it. I need to be grace-filled and forgiving, and I should savor the sweet reward of being understood. Perhaps I should even reflect on the fact that I sometimes "hear" a different message than was intended, and that sometimes the message I "send" is not what is heard.

Like most everything worthwhile in life, good communication requires intention. Sitting in front of the television together or riding in the car with blaring music are not good pathways to understanding. Instead, I'm trying to plan lingering dinners with quiet music or an occasional car trip without *any* music. I need to remind myself to ask lots of questions, and listen intently and without nonverbal evidence of somewhere else to be or something else to do. I have a friend named Grace who embodies this presence like no one else I know. She has three busy children and lots of commitments, but when you are with Grace you'd never get the sense that her time is limited or that she's thinking about the million and one things she needs to do next. I want to be like her. I want to be so present in the moment that my friends feel like I do when I'm with Grace. Such rapt attention is uncommon in our distracted, information-bombarded society. But it doesn't have to be.

For the first eighteen months that we lived in our current house, we had no furniture in our living room. Just recently have we discovered what a lovely room this is. The fireplace and absence of television make it the perfect place to hang out, read and catch up. Whatever happened to living rooms anyway? The great room is great, but the living room is like a safe-haven from media and mindless entertainment. When's the last time you hung out in yours? Does the quiet make you uncomfortable? Because I'm finding this distractionless space to be a wonderful blessing.

I need to periodically remind myself that good communication requires time, intention and effort, just like good relationships. I also need to tell my kindred spirits, my good chemistry pals, how much I need and appreciate them in my life.

THE SIPPY CUP BOMB

If you're a mom, or an aunt, or have friends with kids, you are probably familiar with the drinking device called a sippy cup. It is a plastic contraption that is intended to allow small children to drink out of a cup without spilling. Although preferable to a toddler or preschooler walking around with a bottle, sippy cups are also just plain gross. My boys have all had the bad habit of biting the plastic piece that delivers the liquid, and so the outside looks like it's been put many times over into the garbage disposal, while in truth it won't even fit down there. When I have charming little girls over to my house, who would never dream of such destructive and impolite behavior, they are dismayed by our sippy cup selection.

"Mrs. Jackson," one little darling said, "Do you have any sippy cups that aren't crusty?"

And of course the answer is no, because we are forever losing them, leaving them at church or Bible study or in restaurants or at least once on the roof of a taxi we were climbing into. And then there's the temporary "losing" of sippy cups, in the car, under the bed, down in the couch, in the toy bin, under the train table, in the swim bag, on the back deck. In fact, there are only a handful of places in my house in which a sippy cup has not been "lost," and since the drink of choice for Jackson boys is chocolate milk, a sippy cup hiding for even a few days can acquire a pungent odor. Milk and chocolate curdled together into the valve of a sippy cup is a repulsive sight. And I have unscrewed the cap on some mighty bad sippy cups in my eight years of owning them. So I thought I'd seen it all.

But I hadn't.

One day we had some friends over. There were two boys and a girl, and we'd picked them up from school because their mom was running late, coming from an appointment. Since the house was even more disastrous than usual, I shuffled all six kids into the basement and began straightening up a bit. I don't know where the sippy cup in the sink that fateful day had been. All I know is there has *never* in the history of mankind been a sippy cup like it. I don't know if someone had intentionally contaminated this cup, or if someone in my house had a bacterial infection that took on a life of its own inside the cup or what, but when I unscrewed that cup it was as if a stink bomb had gone off in our house. The stench was like nothing I have ever smelled in my entire life, but was definitely more akin to a baboon than sour milk. Of course, it was at this precise moment that the visiting fourth grader decided to come upstairs and ask for drinks and snacks.

The smell was so bad that I was embarrassed, ashamed even, as if I had somehow emitted or birthed this scent. The young man looked confused and agitated by the overpowering odor, and it was getting worse by the second for me too. I quickly grabbed a bag of pretzels from the pantry. However, since this sweet child has a severe dairy allergy, we needed to ensure there was no trace of milk in the pretzels. He held his nose with one hand, and held the pretzel bag up to his face with the other to read the ingredients.

"Something stinks in here," he said.

"I know," I said apologetically. "It's a nasty sippy cup. Maybe you guys should just stay downstairs. Seriously. It's awful! What the heck?"

"My teacher says you shouldn't say, "What the heck?""

"He does? Okay. Well, I'm sorry. I probably shouldn't. But my gosh, the stench is unbelievable."

"Can I have some juice?" he asked, still holding his nose.

"Sure, sure, sure." I said, starting to panic. I felt like I could actually throw up. And who knows, I could throw up dairy, and any contact with dairy for this little guy could cause a serious reaction.

I whipped open the refrigerator, slamming the things in the door around like an enraged animal, and grabbed the orange juice. Then I grabbed a stack of plastic cups and put them on the counter.

"There you go. There you go. You can take it downstairs," I said hurriedly, hoping to shoo him right out of the kitchen.

But being the responsible, wonderful child that he is, he insisted on reading the orange juice ingredients.

I read it too, over his shoulder, both of us holding our noses for protection.

"Okay, great. No milk. That's great. Okay then," I rambled and off he went with the pretzels, the juice and the cups.

I'm sure any esteem he may have had for me was lost in that little exchange. I'm sure he was thinking, "Her kitchen smells worse than the foulest corner of the dirtiest zoo, she uses pseudo-swear words, and she's impatient!"

I could not figure how this sippy cup managed to continually radiate this unfathomable odor. Did a stink bug die inside the cup? No, I concluded, that would be perfume by comparison. I contemplated that this was some grand conspiracy of neighbor kids involving canine feces or perhaps elephant. Nothing about it looked suspicious, but the smell pointed to intention. I turned on the disposal and doused the sink with Fantastic, rinsing and spraying, rinsing and spraying. I threw the cup in the trash and just as I tied up the bag to take it outside, the mom rang the doorbell.

I washed my hands and answered the door. All six kids were happy in the basement with their pretzels and orange juice, so I explained the sippy cup debacle to my friend. She laughed and laughed, but I think she probably thought I was embellishing the story a bit, especially when I shared my conspiracy theory.

But then as the kids were getting their shoes on and backpacks together, I walked by with the garbage bag to put it in the trash outside.

The mom's face turned slightly pale and quite serious, "Is the sippy cup in that bag?" she asked with visible unease.

As I nodded, grave concern, empathy, and great respect washed over her face. Indeed, this was no mere sippy cup!

But isn't it freeing to have friends who know you, who know you go around bursting dresses at weddings, keeping a messy house, and allowing the creation of the worst smelling sippy cup in world history? It forms such a bond to be found out by someone, to air some of your real self and not feel judged or condemned. This friend does not have toys strewn all over her house, like I do. I've not seen random crayons or an excess of crumbs under her table (not that I've looked). But there is a general sense that she is *not* striving for perfection. One time we had dinner at their house, and when I used the bathroom and washed my hands, there was nothing to dry them on. That gave me joy. I liked flicking the water off my hands, drying them on my pants and smiling over our kindred spirits.

So let us not be pushing our friends into creating facades – domestic or otherwise. And may we not be guilty of creating them ourselves. Being real is the only way to have real friends. And besides, perfectionism is just a joy-robbing scheme of the devil.

JESUS IN A CHAIR

In the fall of 2009 I went away for the weekend, without my family. I stayed in a delightful bedroom that looked out onto the Chesapeake Bay. I slept with the window open, the gentle breeze lulling me into a deep and peaceful slumber. But in the middle of the night, the door to my bedroom flew open. I was startled awake and my heart raced, but then I saw Jesus sitting peacefully in a little wooden chair beside my bed. He wasn't at all concerned about the open door. He was just staring at me.

"Well, if Jesus is here," I thought, "it's probably alright if I just go back to sleep." And so I did. I didn't even bother to close the door.

There are a few things you may want to know before making any judgments about this story. First, the next day, in broad daylight, my door flew open again, but it seemed to be caused by a sudden gust of wind. It was still a little odd, but I think I just didn't have it closed tightly, and the pressure change somehow opened the door. The second thing is that I am a very, very deep sleeper. One time when my husband was working overnight, our security alarm went off in the wee hours. Guess what I did? I stumbled out of bed, made my way over to the keypad and punched in the code to turn it off. Is that funny or what? I was horrified in the morning when I put the pieces of the night together. Thankfully, something other than an intruder had tripped the alarm. The third thing that might be of interest is that I've never before had such a Jesus-sighting.

So honestly, I don't know if I was just tired, scared, or that Jesus was truly visible in that chair. Each is possible and I don't think it matters one iota what really happened. Because what I know in my heart of hearts is that Jesus was there in the room with me, because He is always with me. He told us that He is the Good Shepherd, and He is (John 10). He knows me, and He cares for me. He patiently uses the crook of His staff to guide me; He uses the rod of His staff to shoo away predators. Sometimes my Shepherd leads me beside quiet waters, and He always restores my soul. There is no need for me to fear evil, because He is with me (Psalm 23).

So maybe Jesus was sitting in the chair, or maybe it was a figment of my imagination. Would that be bad? I don't think so. Who gave us our imagination anyway? Do you use yours enough? I'm thinking that maybe I don't. The Psalmists were certainly adept at using theirs. What beautiful word pictures! I am so thankful for all the vivid comfort woven through the Psalms.

And Jesus was constantly using stories and word pictures as tools to teach. He paints the picture of abiding in the vine, of being the right kind of soil, of discerning the Shepherd's voice, of building your house on the rock instead of sand. To fully grasp

Jesus' parables, you must exercise your imagination. If you haven't tried in your mind's eye to picture the father of the prodigal waiting, watching then running – *running* – to his son while he was still a long way off, then you've missed part of the story. We need to get a mental picture of it, because without it, we won't appreciate how desperately the father loved his wayward son. And if you don't understand how much the father loved his wayward son, you probably won't be able to apply the parable to your own life. Because the parable is an illustration of how the God of the Universe loves *you* with a desperate, seeking, unquenchable love no matter how wayward you are.

If you think about it, God could have given us a list of rules to follow, but that's not at all what the Bible is. The Ten Commandments convey basic morality, but they in no way summarize the whole of the Bible, because the Bible is a book of stories. There are a wide range of characters and surprising plot lines. Yet there is also a unified picture of who God is and who we are.

To engage with a story you need a higher order of thinking than to process a list of rules – rules don't require much imagination. Yet sometimes I think professed Christians act like rule people, when the God of the Bible is an undeniable story Person. It's not that rules don't play into stories; of course they do. But rules are a lower order of thinking, and that's not what God intends for us. Jesus told his disciples that they needed to be as shrewd as snakes and as gentle as doves (Matthew 10:16). Knowing rules isn't shrewd. That's not wisdom. Instead, wisdom is knowing the *story* of God's faithfulness, patience and compassion and emulating Him through the power of the Holy Spirit. Of course, in emulating Him more and more you *will* follow all of His rules, but you won't stop there. You'll be living a *more* obedient life than merely checking the box on a list of rules. Rules alone can lead to legalism, but living according to the faith, hope, and love that is illustrated throughout God's Word is inherently mercy and grace-filled. Legalism and condemnation have no place in the life of a believer, because the legalistic and condemning characters in the Bible are presented as clear examples of what not to do.

God gave us the capacity to process stories and not just rules. If we weren't supposed to use our imaginations, He wouldn't have given them to us. And the Bible wouldn't be full of stories either. So we need to use what we've been given. How long has it been since you pictured Jesus in the room with you? Jesus has the most loving eyes, the most willing ear and the most tender heart. Jesus understands us better and loves us more than anyone we've ever known. Living according to these truths is part of the life-changing ministry of Jesus. Maybe it's hard for you to picture the all-loving Person of Jesus in a little chair next to your bed, but picture Him somewhere with you, because with you, He is.

THE NEXT PAVAROTTI

I wrote this essay when Sam was about sixteen months old and we lived in a condo in Falls Church, Virginia. If you met Sam now, this essay would *not* ring true. Now Sam mostly speaks in a soft and gentle voice that's deceivingly sweet. And most of the time he sings in an angelic, embarrassed whisper. I guess if he's going to make a career in opera, he'll have to recover the gusto he possessed as the loudest baby in the world. I decided to leave this essay in the tense that I wrote it because I think it tells the story better than I could tell it now, years after the fact.

My youngest son, Sam, has the loudest cry in the world. And I am not kidding. If there were some kind of loud baby reality show he'd enter and win. I can't imagine any kid even coming close to Sam. People look at me with wild and fearful eyes when he breaks loose in public. His brothers were pretty loud too, but I'd say Sam is about ten times louder than your average loud baby. It's deafening. I'm going to need a hearing aid by the time I'm forty.

The otolaryngologist will probably say, "You've been to a lot of concerts, haven't you?"

And I'll say, "Well, kind of…if you count Sammy's concerts."

What's funny is how some people will continue to talk to me while my little Pavarotti is performing right in my ear. Now, what comes over someone to think that there is any way in the world I could possibly hear them over Sam's cry?

Being the logical and somewhat neurotic person that I am, I assume that whatever message the person is trying to convey to me, it must be very, *very* urgent.

When it is one of Sam's brothers trying to talk to me, I say things like, "Where's the fire?" Or "Who's bleeding?" Then when things settle down, I find out the critical matter was a request for more chocolate milk.

When communication is attempted in the midst of a public scream-fest, I panic even more. "What's that you say? Did you say al-Qaida?" But usually it is something wholly unimportant, at least by comparison, like the fact that Sam is wearing only one shoe.

But Sam's best concerts—where he really shows off in terms of voice projection—are reserved for bedtime and the middle of the night. It is trying indeed for the Jacksons, and yet even worse for our neighbors who share a wall with Sam. I doubt they find much comfort in the fact that Sam has a future or that in his better moments he can charm your socks off. When he's known the world over as Samarotti I don't think they'll be especially proud to have known him before he was famous. I can picture bitter interviews where they recount just how much sleep they lost because of Sam. Does Bose offer those noise-blocking earphones in a sleeping model? Maybe we should give some of those to our neighbors.

I've often wondered why Sam tries to fight off sleep, and with such raucous vim and vigor, even when he's exhausted. And I think what it really comes down to is control. It is hard to give in, hard to submit. The fixation with being in charge of our own destiny is innate—we're born with an "I'm calling the shots" attitude. Think about what a paradox it is that it is *only* when Sam surrenders that he gets what he so desperately needs: sleep.

And the paradox of submission isn't unique to the nursery. The same principle can be observed in other areas of life.

Sometimes it seems that the person who outwardly looks hardest for spiritual answers is the person most reluctant to submit themselves to Christ. They want to be in charge. They want to earn their way. Romans 10:9 states, "That if you confess with your mouth that Jesus is Lord, and believe in your heart that God raised him from the dead, you will be saved." But many people refuse to believe the answer is that simple. They want instead to feel they are working towards something. They want credit for their efforts and take satisfaction in progress made, even if it's fleeting. They cannot accept that Jesus Christ did it all —that salvation is a *gift*. Yet, like Sam it is only in surrender that they are able to receive the free gift Christ is offering them, and like Sam, it's what they need most. But the will is strong, and although surrender is simple, it is far from easy.

Even when someone does confess with their mouth and believe in their hearts the message of the gospel, the struggle with surrender continues. In fact, it's a daily battle. Romans 12:1 tells us that we are to offer ourselves as living sacrifices to God. In other words, we need to submit everything to Him. Everything. So often I want to hold on to one little piece of my life. As if to say, "Lord you take this big chunk of my life. I am making you Lord of all this over here. I'm just keeping this one little part. Can't I be lord of this tiny little corner?" But of course, that's not how it works best. Just like Sam fighting off the sleep his growing body needs, the Christ-followers' unwillingness to submit everything impedes spiritual growth.

A great way to give yourself a spiritual check-up is to ask in what areas are you holding on with a death grip, stubbornly refusing to give them over to the Lord? For me, the hardest thing is my family. I know that God is Sovereign and that He loves me. It makes no sense that I want to hold onto my husband and my boys as if I know better. The absurdity of that! Yet my propensity for control is fierce and surrender is a daily act of the will and a great spiritual discipline. What do you need to surrender today? Why not acknowledge that the All-Knowing, All-Loving Father really does know best?

PRAYING WITH VISION AND PURPOSE

A couple of summers ago, my family was in the midst of fighting some kind of a nasty virus. One night, a little while after Nate went to bed, he started having a terrible coughing fit. You know the kind when the coughing will not subside, and it sounds like there is a real possibility that a lung might come flying out? I rushed into his room, and stood next to his bed. Since he sleeps in the top bunk he is right at eye level for me. I made him sit up, and rubbed his back while he coughed away.

"Aww, sweetie boy," I said, "I'm so sorry you're sick...I'm just going to say a prayer for you right now."

"No, no don't," he yelped between hacks. "It won't work!"

Nate's no-prayer plea is endearing and comical to me now, but in the moment it made my heart sink. Thoughts began rushing through my brain about what was wrong with Nate's picture of God and the purpose of prayer, and I made copious mental notes about the theological concepts we would need to discuss when he was well again. But they would have to wait. We weren't going to address anything too profound right then.

"You know, Nate, " I said, "praying isn't just about getting God to fix things. The Bible says that we are supposed to pray, to tell God what we need, even though He already knows what we need. So I'm going to pray for you right now."

And I did. I prayed that God would allow Nate to stop coughing and get a good night's rest. God graciously answered my prayer. Nate didn't cough at all for hours, and slept peacefully until morning.

When he finally did wake up for the day, I looked forward to talking to him about the true purpose of prayer. I wanted Nate to understand that just because our prayer the night before was mercifully answered just as it was prayed, that God hears and answers all our prayers—whether we see it right away or not. But when I tried to talk to Nate, he didn't remember anything from the night before. Nothing. Zero. Zilch.

My perfect teachable moment was lost in Nate's slumber, yet it got me thinking about prayer—how, what, when, and why we pray.

The quote below was inscribed on an English church in the Eighteenth Century. I think its application is almost universal, and certainly applies to prayer.

A vision without a task is but a dream;

a task without a vision is drudgery;

a vision with a task is the hope of the world.

So if we pray without vision, it will be formulaic drudgery. If we have vision but do not take that vision to the Lord through prayer, it will remain a dream. If we have sanctified imaginations – a vision soaked in prayer – we can change the world. Do you believe in your heart of hearts that prayer effects change? If you don't, why pray? Is it about you? Does it calm your spirit or make you feel "centered?" Because I believe there is incredible, world-changing power in prayer. I do feel calmed and centered by prayer because it helps me focus on my Savior, but there is also great responsibility in knowing that praying to the holy God of the universe changes the course of history. Am I faithful to pray like I really believe that?

The Bible says, "Be joyful always, pray continually, give thanks in all circumstances, for this is God's will for you in Christ Jesus" (1 Thessalonians 5:17).

May we keep the two-pronged vision of doing God's will and being joyful always in mind whenever we pray and give thanks. After all, Jesus is the vision, He demonstrated the task through His earthly life, and He *is* the hope of the world!

MY PRAISE BABY

I would love to be musically inclined. But I'm not. Instead, I have an uncanny ability to forget lyrics and can play exactly one song on the piano: *Pomp and Circumstance*. I played it in a recital at about nine years old and have never forgotten it. But I probably should have recognized my lack of musical gifting at three or four when my Uncle Butch suggested my cousin Cassie and I sing some songs about Jesus. She chose first, and I'm sure she picked some sweet song and sang it right on tune. When it was my turn, I excitedly started with, "Rolling on the River." And no, I do not remember being a young fan of Creedance Clearwater Revival, but evidently I was.

Perhaps I can live vicariously, because Sammy has always been musical. When he was about two weeks old, he started to love Johnny Cash. I'm not kidding. The older boys went to different preschools and so we spent a lot of time driving around. Sam would be screaming his precious little head off and I'd put on Johnny Cash and he'd stop. He even showed a strong preference for "I've Been Everywhere." This despite the fact that our household has a Johnny Cash theme song, "Jackson." If we tried to play "Jackson," Sam would cry and the older boys would plead, "Mom, Mom, put on his favorite, put on his favorite." Only God knows how many times we listened to that song. When Daddy was in the car with us he'd try to play something else, saying, "I'm not going to let my newborn dictate what music I listen to." But eventually he'd give in too. Because you can't really listen to anything when our little Pavarotti is exercising his astounding lungs.

And since Sam was about five months old he loved to watch Praise Baby DVDs. If you've never seen one, they are sort of like Baby Einstein for Christians. The concept is background music and video clips of interesting things to look at, mostly other babies. Of course research has now shown that the Einstein videos are far from genius-inducing, but Sam loved his Praise Baby. And it's hard to believe it was terribly harmful for him to learn to sing all sorts of praise songs when he was just tiny. It has to better than my CCR, right? And he'd get so excited when we heard the songs on the radio, waving his arms and belting out whatever words he knew. One day, when Sam was just two years old, we were driving along when "God of Wonders" came on. That little doll face was overjoyed, and he sang with such passion.

His beautiful little mouth, forming that O-shape to exclaim "holy" was priceless, and while he sang, he sort of swayed back and forth with the rhythm, tilting his head ever so slightly. It was just about the cutest thing I've ever seen.

But the point is that more than being incredibly cute, Sam was unwittingly obeying a biblical command. Because there is a call to sing; it is not a mere suggestion, or a recommendation for those, like Sam, who enjoy music. No, the Psalms repeatedly instruct us to sing. Psalm 33:1 says "Sing joyfully to the LORD." Psalm 33: 3 says "Sing to him a new song." And Psalm 66:1 says "Sing the glory of his name." In fact, there are directives to sing sprinkled throughout the Old and New Testaments.

How often do we sing His praises? We may praise Him in our head, we may even read a psalm of praise, but music is a gift and a command. And it's more about obedience than talent. So may we SING His praises! You will be blessed, and our Loving Father will be glorified.

WHERE ARE OUR ANGELS NOW?

August 7, 2010 was a memorable day for my family –to say the least. We experienced unlikely extremes in that twenty-four-hour period. Elated, then worried. Invigorated and victorious. Then exhausted and helpless.

Each summer my boys compete in the Northern Virginia Swim League. It is a fantastic, efficiently-run league, and my family looks forward to swim season all year. My son, Will, had qualified in two events for the Individual All-Star meet which closes out the season. That beautiful August morning started with 8 and under boys' backstroke. Will was seeded first, which put a lot of pressure on him. It's mentally tough when you are *supposed* to win. Always better to be an underdog. But being the fierce competitor that he is, he swam his heart out and touched the wall first. So at 9:15 a.m. on August 7th, Will was a champion. He had dreamed about this moment, worked hard for this moment, and now he had the satisfaction of seeing it pay off.

And I'm not sure Mrs. Phelps has ever been more proud than I was that morning.

Will swam again that afternoon, placing fourth in the freestyle out of the eighteen all-stars. That race marked the end of an amazing season, but we had no intentions of just relishing the accomplishment or enjoying the downtime of no morning swim practice. Instead, we had reservations beginning that very night at our vacation spot. My husband was working overnight that Saturday and Sunday and would fly to meet up with us on Monday. Sammy fell asleep on the way home from the swim meet, and I let him nap at home, while I removed seats from the minivan and packed it to the gills with bikes and scooters and boogie boards and more clothes and towels and food than we needed. The boys crammed into the bench seat at about six p.m. and we set off. There was no way I could possibly drive all the way to our destination—almost 700 miles – that night. But I figured we'd get as far as we could. This kind of play-it-by-ear planning is so not my husband's modus operandi, but he knew how excited the boys were to get there, so he bid us adieu with lots of kisses and pleas to be careful.

And the trip went quite well. The radio in my minivan was broken and I had not had a spare minute to get it fixed. At the time, we were debating about getting a new minivan anyway. So we used iPods and my iPhone for entertainment, and really Sammy is just like a traveling comedy act so we talked and laughed and made our way through Maryland and Pennsylvania. But as we neared Ohio the boys started to drift off, and an eerie silence and pitch-blackness took over. The eastern end of the Ohio Turnpike is a desolate strip with precious few lights or exits. In fact, I might be forever spooked by Eastern Ohio at night. I had to be careful about not using my iPhone too much because I had no way of charging it. It was almost midnight and I knew it was time to stop. So I started looking at signs and calling a few places. "Booked up," I heard. Booked. Completely Full. Sold Out. "Ma'am, there's nothing until Cleveland because of the golf tournament and the Hall of Fame events." What are the chances that the finals of the World Championships for golf would coincide with the enshrinement of NFL players in Eastern Ohio the one and only night that we needed a room there? I was starting to feel a jittery anxiety, yet my eyes were tired and strained, like I just needed to close them for a couple of minutes.

I called Will at work.

"Can you talk to me until I get to the next exit?" I asked. "It's so dark and so quiet. I'm sort of freaked out."

"Are you gonna fall asleep?"

"No, I'm not sleepy. But it's so dark and so quiet."

I was tremendously proud of him that he didn't say anything like, "See, this is why I don't do things like this." Because I know him, and I know he wanted to.

So we had sort of a strange conversation for about ten minutes or so until I emerged from the perpetual darkness and saw the heartwarming sight of an exit and a Holiday Inn Express. The lady at the counter had the same story for me: "nope, nothing. There's nothing anywhere near here. You could go back to Pittsburgh, maybe."

So I sat in the car with my eyes closed, and Will called around for us from work. The verdict: nothing in Ohio until past Sandusky, meaning at least another 130 miles. But that would be impossible. I just couldn't do it. Too dark. Too quiet. And now I was way too anxious.

So that's how we ended up staying the night in a Holiday Inn Express parking lot.

Those five hours were intense and interesting, and the difference in personalities was magnified. Nate was willing to roll with it. Shockingly, he was almost selfless. He accepted that this was something of a crisis and he did not air a single complaint. Sam was restless and feisty because he'd already taken two substantial naps. He could not get comfortable, no matter how we arranged ourselves. And poor, darling Dub ("Dub" is little Will's nickname, and although I can usually write about him as Will, there are times when the personal nature of the story requires that I use what we actually call him). It was hardest for him. He was the only one who cried, and he yelled out things like, "We are never getting out of here!" and "Where are our angels now?" It makes me laugh to think about it. And even then we had these inexplicable bouts of hysterical laughter. Someone would start laughing and we'd all join in. It was the strangest thing. And Dub, sweet and tender, Dub would go from uproarious laughter to tears and back again. No one slept for an hour or two, because there was this heavy and profound feeling that was just incongruent with sleep. So we talked about God and how we had prayed with Daddy for protection before we left. We talked through questions like, Were we safe? Did God hear our prayer? Were our angels there? Was God in control or not?

I told them that the Bible tells us to pray, but that the Bible also proclaims God's sovereignty. If we think God is like a genie, we will be disappointed. If we think we can produce a certain result by following a certain formula, we will be disappointed.

No, God doesn't want us to be captives of our circumstances, letting our trust ebb and flow with situations we deem good or bad. Instead, He wants us to trust Him in times of victory like that morning, and trust Him in times that are less comfortable, like that night. Our trust, our faith, our love — none of these should be affected by circumstance.

Although I certainly don't intend to set out on another road trip like that one, I do hope and pray that my boys learned to trust God a little more that night. Because I really want to raise three little Davids who can authentically echo the Psalms saying, "Trust in him at all times, O people; pour out your heart before him." (Psalm 62:8).

BAD NAKED AND BAD, BAD NAKED

Do you remember the *Seinfeld* episode about bad naked? Funny that the premise is that there's good naked. Call me prude, but I don't believe it. Now granted, married naked is great naked, but outside of marital intimacy all naked is bad. Like at the gym, I abhor seeing other women naked. It doesn't matter how attractive they are, how young, or how fit, I really just don't want that image in my mind. And some of the least modest women out there are the oldest, so that doesn't help either. But every gym I've ever been to has been like a celebration of nakedness, women having drawn out conversations about everything from the freshness of towels to world peace. I cannot relate. I'm horribly self-conscious and unwilling to undress in front of anyone. My sister, my friends, my mother – no one sees me naked but my beloved.

Actually that's not true. The one other person I get naked in front of is my brother-in-law, Bob, but that's only once every twenty years, and it's certainly not intentional. Well, the first time I guess it sort of was. I was eight or nine years old and with older siblings and not enough bathrooms I wasn't used to having privacy. I guess that's what explains why I did what I did. Anyway, it sounds incredibly weird now, but I used to just get out of the shower, dry off a bit, and then blow-dry my hair, naked. Why didn't I wear a robe? I don't remember owning a robe. Why didn't I at the very least wrap the towel around me? I think I did that, but it always fell down.

So you have to know that when I was eight, my siblings were fifteen, seventeen and nineteen and their friends were in and out of our house at all hours of the day and night. My childhood was vastly different from most. If I couldn't sleep, I'd just go hang out with whatever group of teenagers was gathered in our family room. Surprisingly, I was not made to feel at all like a pest. I could hold a conversation with whomever and knew tons of people twice my age. They had nicknames for me and teased me in good-natured ways. My brother Craig called me "Beeb" which I'm sure was some derivative of "baby" but I don't remember how or why that stuck. But not only did he call me "Beeb" all of the time, but he referred to me as "the Beeb," which I'm sure must have in some way paid tribute to "Leave It to Beaver." He'd come home and ask, "Where's the Beeb?" or if I was sick, "How's the Beeb?" His friends picked up on this, and I'd be walking down the street and have teenagers drive by hanging from the window, yelling "BEEEEEB!" And then one time I was in the drug store with my mom when some dashing teenage boy I'd never seen before asked me, "Are you the Beeb?" It was not your typical childhood. And I was not your typical child. In fact, I was weird.

So weird that one day I was standing there naked blow-drying my hair with the bathroom door wide open when my brother's friend/sister's boyfriend walked by in the hallway. When our eyes met, I was not remotely embarrassed. I didn't close the door like a normal person or yell or anything. Oh no, I just nonchalantly waved with my free hand and called out, "Hi, Bob!"

About four years later, Bob married my sister Laurie, and I was the maid of honor. How many people can say they blew dry their hair naked in front of the groom of a wedding in which they were the maid of honor? Yes, a distinguishing mark on my life for sure. But as much as I dearly love Bob, I never intended to repeat that bad naked moment.

Unfortunately, I can be a slow learner. Locks and doors are wonderful, wonderful things. They should be used! Yet unfortunately when I was twenty-nine years old, Bob and I had another revealing incident, except this one was not just bad naked. It was bad, bad naked. Horrific naked, in fact. When I tell you, if you are a woman, you may tear up - that's how bad it is.

It was October 27, 2001. I was in my closet, once again fresh out of the shower and naked. We had lots of company, but since everyone was downstairs, I didn't think I needed a towel or a robe. I was just standing there searching for something to wear, when in popped Bob. He was shocked and stunned to find me there. He was just looking to borrow one of Will's sweatshirts. Little did he know Will had his own closet.

But what makes this so pitiful is that the reason we had lots of company that day was because on October 22, 2001 – just five days before – my first son was born. I doubt anyone's post-partum body is one they want to share, but it *is* pertinent that I gained sixty pounds and birthed a 7 pound 15 ounce child. Can you imagine the humiliation? Can you grasp the bad nakedness of it?

Of course Bob retreated with eyes shielded, and profuse apologies. And when I talked to him clothed, I thought he might actually cry, he felt so bad about it. I just hope that Bob and I don't have any more twenty-year bad naked reunions.

And although there might be some profound spiritual lesson somewhere in this humbling story, the morals are obvious: lock doors and wear robes.

MORE PHONE CALLS

In January of 2002, I was a new mom and about to turn thirty. In fact, I was still on the maternity leave that my law firm insisted I take when I tried to quit after my son was born.

And although losing my dad had been very difficult, my mom was still my mom. By God's grace, she endured far better than I would have thought possible and she loved spending time with my baby boy. Things were getting better, and I'd planned a ski trip to Park City, Utah. My mom and all my siblings would be meeting us there and I remember Craig saying, "We're gonna have to celebrate the big 3-0 while we are there."

But on January 17th, I received another phone call from my brother Craig. There was a familiar sorrow in his voice and I was immediately filled with dread. He told me that our Uncle Butch -- my mom's brother and my cousin Cassie's dad—had taken his own life. We used our trip insurance and cancelled everything in Utah. We packed up the baby and drove to Michigan instead.

Uncle Butch, whose real name was Wayne, was revered by all his nieces and nephews. He was invested in us, teasing us unmercifully and loving us unconditionally. Since Cassie and I were so close growing up, he was far more than an ordinary uncle to me. He may have been the best listener I've ever known. He didn't even know what it was to half-listen. He was focused in every conversation, like you were the only person in the world. He asked probing questions and knew me better than anyone outside my immediate family. One time when I was about nine, I'd written a story about a princess falling in love with a boy who worked in the barn tending the royal horses. Not the most original story ever written, but I remember Uncle Butch reading my chicken scratch cursive and praising my writing.

"You wrote this?" he asked with feigned disbelief.

"Yes," I answered.

"Are you sure you wrote this? This is fantastic. So well-written. You are talented. I love it. Keep it up."

He was also the kind of person that could make fun out of anything, and that was especially important since I took many, many car trips with Cassie and her family. We drove to Florida for most Easter vacations and to my grandparents' farm, an hour away, with great frequency. I've never been able to sleep or read in the car so Uncle Butch was my around-the-clock source of entertainment. He told me great stories about growing up. There were four siblings in all, but Uncle Butch and my mom were a dynamic duo, riding their horses like the characters on The Lone Ranger and Kit Carson, two of their favorite TV shows. One time Uncle Butch rode his horse and pulled the reins to my mom's horse as fast as he could and as close as he could beside the chicken house. My mom was perched on top and jumped off onto her horse. They had some wild times and horror of horrors there were no helmets!

My uncle was a high school history teacher and when I'd meet someone who went to that high school, I'd always ask, "Did you know Mr. Cummins?" The response was invariably the same. "Oh, he was my favorite teacher of all-time!" I know he was dedicated, that he loved his subject matter, and that he made history fun and exciting, but I think the real magnetism of Wayne Cummins was the fact that he made everyone feel special—it was that focused attention, that loving encouragement that came so naturally to him.

But in his early fifties Uncle Butch started to experience dramatic mood swings. He was eventually diagnosed with bipolar disorder.

In the fall of 2000, Uncle Butch and his son, Clay (who is nine years younger than Cassie and me), visited us in DC. My uncle was in the midst of a mild episode of mania. I remember him talking ninety miles per hour and although much of what he said was quite funny, it left you with sort of unsettled feeling, because it was just over-the-top.

The last time I saw him was at Christmas of 2001, just a month before he died. I was so excited for him to meet my newborn son. But those engaging, piercing blue eyes of his were distracted. The easy conversationalist was gone; he showed almost no interest in my son and wore a blank and unfamiliar look. I remember him asking my husband, "So who do you think will win the Super Bowl?"

His question came across as a strained attempt at normalcy, but there was no masking his disheartening transformation.

In some respects, mental illness is a disease like any other, yet after a suicide the family grapples not just with the loss, but with the feeling that their loved one chose to leave. Of course it was a great comfort to all of us that my uncle had long known and loved the Lord Jesus.

It was six months later that another heartbreaking telephone call came in, except this one was not from my brother, Craig; it was about my brother, Craig.

It was July 20, 2002 and my mom was in town for a visit. It was a Saturday, Will was home, and we were all playing with the baby. My mom had gone downstairs and the call came in on her cell phone. She cried out and I went running downstairs to see what was the matter. Will was right behind me. The call was from my brother's wife and she explained that Craig had been in a small airplane that had gone down that morning in the Atlantic Ocean. The Coast Guard had reported that there were no survivors.

This struck me immediately as too much. I couldn't lose my brother too, and neither could my mom. I tried to rationalize that he was such a good swimmer, maybe they were mistaken, maybe we'd soon hear that he was safe after all. I went for a "drive" in the car because what I really wanted to do was scream my head off and ask God, "Why?" But screaming and begging didn't help, and we didn't get the good news I'd hoped we might.

The next morning the four of us – my mom, my husband, my son and I – took the first flight to Palm Beach where Craig lived. We sat in one row. I was between my mom and my husband with baby boy on my lap. We were stunned. We talked very little and Will had tears streaming down his face the entire flight. Craig had meant so much to each of us. He'd been a wonderful and attentive son, a protective and loving brother, and for Will, a best friend.

Craig had not yet had any children of his own, but had always had a way with kids. He had early practice with little cousins and a baby sister, and our niece, Caitlin, and nephew, Dane, adored him. Even their friends lovingly called him "Uncle Craig." The month before Craig's death, when my oldest was about seven months old, he had visited us and delighted over his brutishly big nephew, showering him with hugs and kisses. The last day I spent with Craig, it was just Craig, Baby Dub and me, because Will was working. We hung out at the pool and Craig cracked up over Dub's fearlessness in the water. We took turns dunking him and marveling that a baby could love the water that much. Another time we'd been at that pool, Craig was a few pounds – well, maybe thirty or so pounds -- above his ideal weight. After doing a few flips and one-and-a-halfs off the diving board, a group of kids began to gather round. Shy at first, they asked if he could help them. Craig spent the next hour giving impromptu lessons and pointers to the crew assembled. This was not an uncommon phenomenon – he had such a magnetic and kind spirit about him. As a professional golfer he had a knack for instruction, and the littlest golfers always flocked to him.

That day as we walked to the car I said, "Wow, those kids sure did love you."

Craig shrugged and quipped, "Well sure, I'm the best *fat* diver they've ever seen."

The memorial in Florida and the funeral in Michigan were impressive outpourings of love for my brother. Anyone who knew Craig knew he loved the Lord, and these services were Christ-centered, just as he would've wanted.

Looking back, I see how divinely orchestrated my life is, and how important it was for me to already be a mother when I lost my brother. My son needed me, and I couldn't just wallow in self-pity. Instead, I had this precious, adorable, amazing little guy who brought joy to my life even in the midst of great sorrow. It's not that new joys replace old ones. I still miss my brother terribly, and I often have imagined conversations with him because we had so many inside jokes and movie lines at the ready. I often know exactly what he would say if he were sitting next to me, and so I still laugh about so many things because of him. Plus, although some people are fond of the generic, "they're in a better place," I *know* Craig is in heaven. He can never be hurt or disappointed or heartbroken again. He'll never get another heart-wrenching phone call, nor will he have to make one. Instead he is with the loving Creator of the Universe. And someday I'll join him.

GRAND THEFT AUTO

When I was fifteen years old, I stole a car. Actually, I think the legal term for it is joyriding. I had no intention of keeping the car, and such intention is a necessary component for theft. But the proper definition has long been ignored in my family. For over two decades, the story of Kristie stealing a car has been retold.

Melissa is one of my oldest and dearest friends, and one Saturday night in November of 1987, we were hanging out at her house. Her parents were out for the night, and we were talking about a boy we used to like quite a bit. But that was *weeks* before, and now there was a hint of vengeance in the air. There is no explaining the utter stupidity of it, but I proposed grabbing a couple of eggs and taking her parents car for a little drive over to his house, maybe three miles away. Melissa needed convincing. For whatever reason, she did not think this was the best idea in the whole world, like I did. But I'm a good salesperson, and before long I was backing her parents' car from the driveway, and Melissa was in the passenger's seat holding the eggs. This despite "I wouldn't do that if I were you" sentiments and looks from Melissa's two younger siblings.

Everything was going swimmingly as we exited her neighborhood. But then we came to a four-way stop, and wonder of wonders, a police car pulled up across from us. His presence caused me to stammer, to utterly panic. We had been intending to turn left, but now I thought maybe we should turn right. I flipped the turn signal up and down and then up again, and well, it was pretty suspicious-looking. And then when I did finally turn right I doubt it was my turn. So we made it about a quarter of a mile from her house before a police car was on my bumper with lights flashing. It sounds pathetic, but I remember thinking that perhaps something more pressing could divert the police. Maybe someone could zoom by right then going like 75 in a 25 and certainly that would be more important than suspicious four-way stop behavior. But that thought was short-lived, and I pulled the car over terrified and resigned to what felt like a fate worse than death.

Minutes later we were in the back of the caged cruiser and Melissa was practically hyperventilating. The proclamation that the car would be impounded did not lift our spirits! I remember begging the officer to please just leave the car where it was, safely parked on a side street around the corner from its rightful owner. I even told the officer that I was sure it would be alright if he just drove it back to their house. But my begging was futile. We drove Melissa home and then the police escorted me to my sister's house about five or so minutes away. The officers were skeptical of my story. But it was true. My parents were out of town and I really did live with my sister while our new house was being built.

I don't know when I started crying. I do not think I cried much, if at all, while Melissa was there. But the closer we got to my sister's house, the harder I cried. She'd be disappointed. Her husband would be disappointed. And we'd eventually have to tell my parents, a thought I could not think without shuddering. So with each mile, I was getting more and more out of control. When the police opened the back door of the cruiser, set to walk me to the door, I was completely hysterical. I was wailing like I'd been shot. My poor sister's first thought was that I'd been sexually assaulted. I mean it does make sense with the police escort and all. So she was ecstatic to learn, with that frame of mind, that the issue was merely a stolen car. I'd given her such a scare that she was downright thrilled by my thievery.

But telling my parents was not so easy. I enlisted my brother Craig for moral support. He agreed to be there with me, but insisted that I do the actual telling. And I didn't tell my dad. I told my mom, and she told my dad. I despised the feeling of disappointing them, yet that possibility didn't cross my mind when I was grabbing the keys and climbing into the car.

I remember my dad dropping the check off at Melissa's house for the impound fee. I was humiliated and felt like I never wanted to see her family again. I was too ashamed. They had been *so* good to me, and this is what I did in return. Surely, my transgression was unforgiveable.

But after about two weeks, which seemed an eternity, her dad called me on the phone. It was a Sunday afternoon in early December.

"Kristie, Honey," he said, "We want you to go to the mall with us. We miss you."

"Okay," I answered, voice quivering.

A half hour later, their family of five picked me up at my sister's house. I piled in, feeling something like a sewer rat.

There must have been some exchange involving, "I'm sorry," but I don't remember that. What I do remember is laughing until my face hurt. At every intersection all the way to the mall, her dad did a Kristie, flipping the turn signal up and down and then up, acting like a panicked goof.

What a beautiful and uncommon picture of forgiveness!

Jesus said, she who has been forgiven much loves much (Luke 7:47). And I love that family. Oh, how I love them. They were always, always so good to me. They took me on vacations, opened their home to me, and encouraged me and loved me. But nothing made more of an impression on me than their willingness to forgive me. How many kids have people outside their own family who are that *for* them?

This experience, while obviously quite embarrassing, taught me a wealth of life lessons. Looking back I can see God's protective hand in getting caught. I see the power of investing in my children's friends, of sharing with them the blessing of forgiveness and of being in their corner. And I see living proof of many biblical truths like the fact that forgiveness engenders great love, that kindness leads to repentance, and that wisdom is learning from mistakes.

So often God uses everyday life and everyday stories to illustrate spiritual truths about Himself and His creation. The love that I have for this family -- this heartsick love of gratitude—should be just a hint of the love that we have for God. Because He has forgiven everything we've ever done. He has never run out of patience or given up on us and He never will. As Paul so aptly wrote in Romans, " If God is for us, who can be against us?" (8:31).

Do you wake up each morning confident that God's mercies to you are brand new? That He is *for* you every step of the way? That He is never giving up on you, no matter how many cars you've stolen or how many stupid mistakes you continue to make? This is what God wants for you. He wants you to embrace his undying, unconditional love. He wants you to know you are forgiven and loved eternally through the sacrifice of His Son. The question is, do you? Do you know His peace? Or are you striving for something else, some achievement that is yours alone? Look around you. Do you know people who walk *closely* with the Lord Jesus? People who cast an undeniable light in a dark world, people who live with a peace that passes understanding, people who forgive willingly and love recklessly?

An even more important question: Am I this kind of person?

THERE *IS* NO OTHER WAY

In 1887, a hymn was penned that may provide the simplest and best synopsis of the entire Bible ever put to music. I encourage you to Google "Daniel Towner," "John Sammis" and the title "Trust and Obey." This hymn by John Sammis has an interesting inspiration that is well worth your time, and it conveys a profound truth in a simple, almost C.S. Lewis-esque way.

Trust and obey, for there's no other way

To be happy in Jesus, but to trust and obey

Yet as familiar as these lyrics are, many Christians give Christianity a bad rap by ignoring the call to obedience. As Gandhi famously quipped, "I like your Christ, I do not like your Christians. Your Christians are so unlike your Christ." What a heartbreaking, sincere and often accurate observation!

But the lack of obedience doesn't merely impair the believer's role as an ambassador for Christ, it impedes personal peace. To be happy you need to trust Jesus and obey Him. Contrary to the implicit message sent by the lifestyles of many "Christians," trusting and obeying are not mutually exclusive. Instead, Dietrich Bonhoeffer argued that these two elements are like two points on a self-reinforcing circle. The more you trust, the more you are able to obey, and the more you obey, the more you are able to trust. Sometimes we need to exercise our will and choose to trust Him. Even if we are not motivated by love, even when we really don't want to, we are called to obey anyway. Feelings come and go, but a spiritual life dependent on emotion will be one lived in defeat. We need to know that sometimes – maybe even oftentimes, during certain seasons of life – it's necessary to choose to trust and choose to obey in spite of our circumstance and emotional state.

Marriage is like this too. Most days I am enraptured by my husband. Will is funny. He's smart and he loves Jesus. We have more than twenty years of inside jokes, and no earthly being refreshes my soul, and entertains me and understands me like Will does. But there are times when we can rub each other the wrong way. In many respects we are night and day. He's organized and disciplined. I'm scatterbrained and indulgent. Our differences provide a healthy balance for our two extremes. But our differences can also be abrasively irritating. If our marriage wasn't based on commitment, we'd be doomed. In fact, I believe all marriages which are founded upon emotions and physical attraction are destined to fail, and of course there's ample evidence that neither emotions nor attraction are sustaining for the long-term. However, the biblical institution of marriage is a life-long commitment, based on forgiveness and the call to love and respect one another.

It's folly to follow Jesus based purely on emotion, because even though emotions are often real and wonderful, just like they are in marriage, feelings are also unreliable. We need an unshakable foundation, one not subject to whims or moods. We need love and truth, just like in marriage. There are times when you must choose to love your spouse, and you must choose to never give up. There are times in a life of faith, where volitional trust and volitional obedience are vital. Sometimes love is an act of the will. Sometimes faith is an act of the will too.

Of course, I'm not talking about checking boxes. You can't check the "I didn't cheat on my spouse" box and think that's enough. You can't check the "I provided basic shelter and nourishment for my family" box and think that's enough either. The Bible doesn't outline minimum standards. The bar is always high. Jesus explained that murder includes hateful thoughts, and adultery includes lusting after anyone not your spouse. But duty in the Old Testament was always more than box-checking. In Micah 6, we see the nation of Israel essentially asking the Lord what then shall we do? And the Lord answers through His prophet: "He has showed you, O man, what is good. And what does the Lord require of you? To act justly and to love mercy and to walk humbly with your God."

We are mistaken then to think about obedience as a list of rules. It's a much higher calling than rule following. The Lord requires that we act justly, love mercy and walk humbly with Him. So how are you doing on those? Are you just? How does the unjust treatment of others in your neighborhood or around the world affect you? Do love mercy? Even for those who have wronged you and hurt you deeply? Do you walk humbly with God? Do you marvel that He is mindful of you?

For me, these questions are humbling, grounding and convicting. Yet, what a great way to assess our spiritual health. Be honest about how justly you act, how deeply and truly you love mercy, and how humbly you walk with the Lord.

May we trust and obey the Lord Jesus, the author and perfecter of our faith, with steadfast and Spirit-empowered devotion, because John Sammis was right, there *is* no other way to be happy in Jesus.

SURRENDER

When I was about five or six years old, I prayed with my mom to accept Jesus as my Savior. It was sweet relief to believe that I would go to heaven when I died. My faith was simple and pure, and I am thankful that God heard my prayer. Yet I did precious little to grow my faith, praying now and then, reading a devotional here and there, and on rare occasions cracking open His Word. Far from being a devoted follower of Christ, I marched through the next couple decades, with eternal security in hand, living life my own way.

It wasn't until I got married that I began to realize how unanchored my life really was. My husband exceeded my wildest expectations in every way and I was crazy about him, yet somehow marriage wasn't easy. It may have seemed like a fairy-tale from the outside, but on the inside there was a palpable absence of pixie dust. He was human and flawed. And I was human and very flawed. But in retrospect, our imperfections were a blessing. They made reality clear. My love for Will was imperfect, as was his love for me. Yet I had a longing, even a need for perfection. I desperately wanted someone who would never disappoint me, who would love me into being a better person, a forgiving person, and a more loving person. As I began to truly study the Bible for the very first time in Bible Study Fellowship, I realized that I had been loved like this all along. Jesus had patiently and faithfully pursued me even when I accepted his saving grace and rejected his guiding hand.

At eighteen, I was baptized in the church where I grew up. I confessed Jesus as my Savior that day, yet in retrospect I don't know how serious I was about my faith at all. Maybe it's natural to look back twenty years and be stunned by the difference. But it is not the case that I've just grown closer to the Lord; it is not the case that I'm more mature, with a greater appreciation for biblical truth. Spiritually, I'm just a different person with a different heart, and so I've thought many times about being re-baptized.

As Romans 10:9 states: "That if you confess with your mouth that 'Jesus is Lord,' and believe in your heart that God raised him from the dead, you will be saved." I couldn't say Jesus was my Lord in 1990, but by God's grace, twenty years later, I can. And that's why on August 12, 2010 I was re-baptized at sunset in beautiful Lake Michigan. It was a wonderful celebration with many fellow believers standing on the sand, many of whom I am related to in one way or another. It was also incredibly meaningful because of who was standing next to me in the lake: my eight-year-old-son, Will. I am praying that his young baptism will mark his life in a profound way. I know he trusts Jesus as his Savior, and I believe he is serious about making Jesus Lord over all.

I realize the Christian life is a process and not just a one-time event, but I think it's possible to overemphasize process and discount the true value of one-time declarations. Saying the words "I do" in my wedding ceremony changed my whole life and my legal standing. Accepting a job offer is life changing, as is committing to playing on a team. These are things that happen at a moment in time, and yet also have an ongoing component.

Proclaiming Jesus as Savior is a one-time declaration, but also involves the ongoing recognition that you are totally unable to save yourself. In 2006, I realized for the first time how this same principle applies to making Jesus your Lord. Will and I were attending a weekend Bible conference in Asheville, North Carolina. The pastor was teaching that weekend out of Romans 12, and on that Sunday morning he was wrapping up his remarks by reviewing, in part, what it means to live a life fully surrendered to God. Romans 12:1 says: "Therefore, I urge you, brothers, in view of God's mercy, to offer your bodies as living sacrifices, holy and pleasing to God—this is your spiritual act of worship." I'd never before considered the verb tense used in this familiar verse. Interestingly, in the Greek, the verb tense means something that is ongoing, but also something that happens at a point in time. The ongoing part didn't surprise me – I knew submission was a process. After all, surrender doesn't come naturally, and we need to declare that Jesus is Lord everyday.

But what struck me—what the pastor so artfully pulled out – was that this surrender also happens at a point in time. And it's not when you initially give your life to Christ. In other words, this verse is asking you to make a one-time, all out surrender. We may rationalize that we can never attain perfect surrender because it's a journey. And of course it is a journey. But it is also a moment. A moment between you and God where you commit to Him, not for the sake of your salvation, but for the sake of Christ's Lordship in your life. Have you made that kind of commitment? Or is there something or someone you've held back?

On October 22, 2006, I prayed and told God something like this: Here it is. Here's my whole life. There is nothing I want to keep from you, Lord. Not my family, not my comfortable lifestyle, not anything, Lord. You are Lord over *all* of it. I am submitting everything – everything to you. I know living a fully surrendered life will mean opening my hand to You again and again, that I have this propensity to resolve, "Not this, Lord" or "Anything but that, Lord." But in this moment, I am letting go of the things I hold onto so tightly –especially my family. I am surrendering it *all* and trusting Your plan for my life.

Have you ever done that? Have you ever just declared Jesus Lord over all? I hope that if you haven't, you'll take a few minutes to do that right now because I believe God's peace that passes understanding and the freedom for which He set us free are found, paradoxically, in surrender.

More than six hundred years ago, Thomas a Kempis wrote on surrender from the perspective of our heavenly Father:

If you resign yourself wholly into my hands, and take back nothing for yourself, you will have more grace from Me...Some people resign themselves to Me, but with some reservation, for they do not fully trust Me, and therefore study to provide for themselves; and some at the beginning offer all to Me, but afterwards, when any temptation comes, they turn again to their own will and to what they promised to forsake, and therefore they gain little in virtue...I have said to you many times before, and I say to you yet again, forsake yourself wholly to Me, and you will have great inward peace."

Are peace, freedom and grace indelibly marked on your life? I hope so.

HARAKA HARAKA HAINA BARAKA

I have some very dear friends, Nancy and Lindsay, who recently traveled to South Africa. They came home with many wonderful stories, incredibly beautiful photographs, and a vision for helping a village they visited called Lilydale, which is in Kruger National Park. In this small village, a woman named Maggie had started a school for children with disabilities just a few years ago. Maggie felt called to found this school after she had prayed and asked God for a purpose in life. Not long after, a woman from her church asked if Maggie would be willing to care for a child with disabilities, so that the parents could work during the day. When Nancy and Lindsay visited in the fall of 2010, they met Maggie and toured her school, Tshemba Hosi. The name means "Love and Peace," and when they visited, Tshemba Hosi was caring for over 120 disabled children and young adults.

Nancy and Lindsay shared with their Bible study about Maggie and the children. As a Christmas present, the group gathered two hundred pounds of clothes, toys, and books and shipped them to Maggie and her students. I loved hearing about their trip and how it affected them, but the biggest take-away for me personally was a Swahili saying they learned while they were there: haraka haraka haina baraka." It means simply, "hurry hurry has no blessings."

And hurrying is a struggle of mine. Just the other day, I was hurrying from one good thing to another. I left Bible study, where I was awed and inspired by elementary kids who undoubtedly know the Bible better than the vast majority of Americans, and was on my way to supervise recess at my boys' school. But in that brief drive from one place to the next, and feeling a little short on time, I rear-ended the unsuspecting driver in front of me.

On the one hand, these things happen. Not that long ago, I was involved in a strange and unlikely fender-bender. The boys and I were on a side street, waiting to turn right, when the woman in front of us put her car in reverse and backed into us. I guess she thought the nose of her car was sticking out into traffic. We both got out of our cars, and this break-taking, middle-aged Asian woman, was very upset even though there was no real damage.

"Oh, I'm so sorry," she said, arms flailing in distress. "Sun so bright."

"That's okay, " I said. "Look, there's no damage. It's not a big deal."

But then she saw that I had the boys in the car, and she almost lost it: "Oh, and you have children! Oh, I'm so sorry, so, so sorry."

I assured her that they were fine, but this did not ease her angst, so finally I just hugged her. My middle son thought that was the strangest thing in the world, but it did seem to help. A few minutes later we were back in our cars and drove off.

Unfortunately, the Norwegian that I rear-ended did not hug me. He was kind enough, and he probably didn't know that I would have been very receptive to a brief little, "It's going to be alright" hug!

But the accident was just the beginning! It was merely the impetus of a long, long lesson of haraka haraka haina baraka. Since my van was almost nine years old, had suffered quite a bit of damage in the accident, and had racked up a ton of miles, we knew it was time to put her down. The next day I started researching new minivans and narrowed it down to two. Later that afternoon I test-drove the first option and when I saw the bottom line, I felt good about going ahead with it. However, by the time the paperwork was done, it was 5:20 pm and my husband had to work at 7:00 pm. I needed to get out of the dealership and get home so Will could leave for work. However, it had started to snow and I was getting more and more nervous about driving a brand new minivan home in slick conditions. After all, it had only been about thirty hours since I'd rear-ended my Norwegian friend.

My salesman, being a kind and generous man, offered to drive me home. Looking outside at huge and continuous snowflakes and the three inches that had already accumulated, I took him up on it. Neither of us could have predicted what we were getting into. That night proved to be one of the worst traffic disasters in Capital area history. Many commuters spent twelve hours or more getting home, and an hour later, we had made precious little progress in our six-mile trip. I hated to tell Will that he'd have to pack up the boys and head to work, but that was our only option. We'd have to meet up there or else he'd have to be late for work.

After another half hour or so, we ended up in front of a Chick-Fil-A. My new friend was getting hungry and I was incredibly thirsty, so we hit the drive-thru. I ordered food for my whole family and downed my large Diet Coke in no time. But that proved to be an extremely foolish indulgence, because for hours, we mostly did not move. When the car rolled for more than ten feet it was like an adrenalin rush, "Ahhh, progress!" And of course, the Diet Coke was the primary factor, but I think nervous anxiety exacerbated how badly I needed to use the restroom. For hours, I felt like I might wet my pants. I wished I'd followed in the footsteps of Lisa Nowak. Her planning seemed brilliant and entirely reasonable.

My friend offered to pull over, and angle the car to ensure privacy, but I could not bring myself to do that. Instead, I sat there jittery-legged and miserable, breathing mostly Lamaze style. My new friend was becoming so dear. He was so kind and gracious, and I thoroughly enjoyed talking with him. We covered many bases—from favorite restaurants to favorite sports teams, from Jesus to government handouts, from vocations to vacations, from having kids to having heart attacks. If you spend that much time with someone it's almost impossible not to like them. It's a corollary of haraka haraka haina baraka: take your time, take your time, and you will be blessed.

108

But I was still *desperate* to get out of his car. After more than three hours, we rolled up an exit ramp and stores were just a hundred feet to our right. It was clear that it'd be another twenty minutes or so before we were off the ramp, able to merge into traffic and turn right into the shopping center. But I couldn't wait another twenty minutes. I had to jump out. The problem was that between us and the stores was a wall about four or five feet high, and a fence on top of the wall about six feet tall. It looked daunting, especially since it was blizzard conditions and I had no coat, hat or gloves. But I really felt like I had to try it. I had to get out of the car. As I approached the wall, I spotted an opening in the fence. Now all I had to do was get on top of the wall. I tried to pull myself up by grabbing onto the fence, but I couldn't do it.

I prayed, "Please, God let me climb this wall," and right then I spotted a street sign that had a sort of tripod base, next to the wall. I thought maybe I could use that as leverage. It worked beautifully and it felt like a great victory to be on top of the wall. But now I was about twenty-five feet from the opening in the fence so I had to scoot along the wall, hanging on to the fence. When I made it to the opening I just started praising Jesus, and I praised Him every step of the way to Starbucks. Just as I was approaching the power flicked off, and when I got to the door I could see a sign saying Starbucks had closed. Next door was a little Vietnamese restaurant, although the lights were still off, I could see the silhouettes of people sitting at tables inside. I entered, covered in snow and looking like a lunatic. I made my way through the dark restaurant toward the back. I was sure the restroom would be pitch black, but I didn't care. I was more than willing to feel my way around or use my cell phone as a flashlight. But halfway back the lights came on and a bewildered, but polite waiter asked, "Take out order?"

I didn't even break my stride. I just mumbled, "oh, on the way out, on the way out."

The Bible says to give thanks in all circumstances (1 Thessalonians 5:18), but I'd never in my life given thanks for a restroom like I did that night. On the way out, I ordered a Thai iced tea, because I felt like I had to order something! I paid and took my time making my way over to the entrance of the shopping center. After a few minutes, my friend pulled in. I'm sure he was wondering what in the world I was doing consuming another beverage! I thanked him profusely, grabbed the two bags of Chick-Fil-A and said good-bye. Then I made my way over to Will's work, which was just about a block away, yet seemed longer without a coat.

I was there for ninety minutes before my family arrived. Their three-mile trip had taken almost four hours. Instead of getting back in the car, the boys and I just slept at Will's work that night. It was like a bring-your-family-to-work event for the nocturnally employed.

I liked the phrase haraka haraka haina baraka as soon as I heard it, but it now means even more to me. I hope that I won't soon forget the lessons that I learned in those thirty-six hours, which were many. Most of all, may I not hurry past the blessings God intends for me, and may I be grateful in all circumstances!

BEAUTY FOR ASHES, WREATHS FOR STICKS

For the last couple of years I've had this same wreath on my front door. There is something pretty and simple about it; it's the kind of décor I really enjoy, the kind I never tire of. It recently occurred to me, for the first time, that the wreath is actually made of sharp sticks! It could be easily replicated by taking some sharp, yet malleable, sticks, forming them into an imperfect circle, and then adorning with little flowers.

And life is not unlike that wreath—we all experience heartaches and disappointments, embarrassing situations and regrettable moments. I've shared many of my own sharp sticks on these pages, but the wonderful news is that God never wastes anything. I am impressed by friends who are faithful and efficient at recycling and reusing, of making beautiful creations from what others might throw away. I am inspired when someone takes leftovers and produces a gourmet meal. But God is not like them—He doesn't waste little, He wastes nothing! Every mountaintop experience and every visit to the valley will be used by God. We have to be malleable. We need to trust and submit to His good, pleasing and perfect will. We need to acknowledge that we are sinners and that we have no intrinsic right to be with a holy and perfect God, and accept the sacrifice that Jesus Christ made on our behalf. But if we do that, if we just answer His call, we are promised that what God has begun in us He will complete (Philippians 1:6). We can rest in the confidence and peace that for those who love Him, God works all things for good (Romans 8:28). Isaiah poetically describes this idea that nothing is irredeemable – Jesus bestows crowns of beauty, instead of ashes (Isaiah 61:3).

If we trust in the tapestry that He is weaving in our lives, one day we'll be amazed by a beauty we cannot now see. But trusting in this ultimate tapestry—or this wreath that God is forming through the sharp sticks in your life –is not at all like taking the lemons life hands you and making lemonade. Because this is not an endeavor for you alone. It is partnering with the God who loves you so much that He sent His only Son to die for you. It is embracing a biblical worldview. It means studying God's Word, seeking relationship with Jesus Christ, serving Him, emulating His life, and relying with faith and hope on His provision, His love and His plan.

I want my life to be one that manifests faith in and obedience to Jesus Christ. I want to live with joy and gratitude and to glorify my God in all I do. I hope that no matter how sharp the stick, I will trust that God knows what He is doing. Because I believe the path to freedom is paved by radical faith and radical obedience. Paradoxically, submitting to the Lord of the Universe is the most liberating thing you can do with your life. It may seem illogical to outsiders, but I've witnessed over and over again that the people who are the most joy-filled, the people who live life to its fullest, the ones who love the most recklessly, who forgive the most easily, who enjoy the greatest peace—they all have something in common. They are committed and submitted to Jesus Christ. Please note that I did not say the most affluent, the most well-travelled, the most well-read, the most successful, the most powerful, or the most outwardly attractive. None of these things are bad, and some sold-out believers that I know are all of these things as well, but these things can also be stumbling blocks on the road to truth. We are often hard of hearing and nearsighted until we encounter despair. The fun and busyness of life may keep us from searching for answers to our deepest questions and longings. But the mysteries of purpose, meaning and destiny become too great when life is hard. Sometimes it is what at first appears unbearably difficult that God uses to bless us immeasurably.

My hope and desire is that the stories in this book have caused you to contemplate the love of Jesus Christ and what YOU will do with it. My fervent prayer is that you will accept the gift that Jesus lovingly offers you, and that you too will commit to living a life of faith in and obedience to Him.

JILL'S HOUSE

I knew I wanted to give a portion of the proceeds of this book to a ministry or charity. When I was praying about which organization to give to, I kept feeling led to Jill's House, which is a ministry that provides respite for families who have children with special needs. Will and I prayed about how much to give, and decided that half of the author proceeds should go to Jill's House. I contacted Jill's House in beginning of December of 2010, and have felt great confirmation in this decision through a series of interesting and unlikely events.

However, nothing could have convinced me that I'd made the right choice like visiting Jill's House in February of 2011. I was expecting it to be beautiful. I was expecting it to be wonderfully and thoughtfully designed. After all, I've seen pictures and I've watched the time-lapsed video of it being built. But my grandiose expectations fell pitifully short. Jill's House provides a fantastic opportunity for parents to get a reprieve from caring for their child with special needs, but when you visit the facility, it conveys a spirit that is all about loving the kids. I visited the art room, stocked with inspiring supplies, and the music room, full of instruments with plenty of room to dance. There are themed sensory rooms with things to touch and marvel at. Children love the bubbling cylinders, neon lights, disco balls, and soft, life-size blocks with which to build forts. There is a swimming pool built with special needs in mind, and the water sparkles with all of the natural light streaming in from an abundance of windows.

The decor of Jill's House is inviting, looking much like a resort. Many of the interior walls are painted with thematic murals — tropical scenes in the pool area, space and wilderness scenes in the common areas near the bedrooms. The playground is almost entirely shaded and is accessible and fun for children in wheelchairs and also children who can run and swing from monkey bars.

It was a battle for me not to cry happy tears while touring Jill's House. It was overwhelming. I just kept thinking about how much it must mean to the families served by this incredible facility. Think of all the parents (many of them undoubtedly single parents) reaching a point of utter exhaustion caring for their child with special needs, and then having the opportunity to bring them to Jill's House. What a blessing for the parents and for the child!

I am thrilled that every time someone buys *Sharp Sticks* a donation will be made to this fantastic and much needed ministry. God instructs us to love everyone with the eyes of Christ. It is His truth that we are all made in His image, worthy of respect and dignity and love. God is never about outward appearances or tangible contributions. He is always and only about grace (Romans 3:24, 2 Corinthians 12:9, Ephesians 2:8, and Titus 2:11).

Likewise, Jill's House is a place of grace and love, of rest and fun, a place where children are honored and respected and cherished regardless of ability or appearance. A kingdom mindset — a theology in action — that is all too rare.

AUTHOR'S NOTE

I am humbled and honored that you would take the time to read *Sharp Sticks*, I am thankful for your contribution to Jill's House (www.jillshouse.org), and I would love to hear from you. You can connect with me through my website (www.kristieejackson.com), where I post weekly on my blog, *Spur*.

Made in the USA
Charleston, SC
30 October 2011